Navigating Data Protection

A Straightforward Roadmap to Compliance

By

Paul Byrne

Disclaimer

This book is intended to provide general guidance on data protection and compliance. It does not constitute legal advice and should not be relied upon as such. Readers should seek independent legal counsel where specific legal interpretation or advice is required.

Every effort has been made to ensure that references to legislation and regulatory requirements, including the Articles of the Data Protection (Jersey) Law 2018 and any other laws cited, are accurate at the time of writing. However, readers are strongly advised to verify all legal references, as amendments, revisions, and updated guidance are common.

Compliance with data protection regulation is a continual process. It evolves as laws develop, regulatory expectations shift, and organisational practices change. No book, tool, or framework can guarantee full compliance. What this text aims to offer is a practical starting point, helping you to understand the landscape and begin, or continue, your journey toward stronger compliance.

Use this book as a roadmap, not a destination. The responsibility for ensuring adherence to the law rests with you and your organisation. Approach the material critically, adapt it to your context, and keep learning.

Good luck on your quest to navigate data protection well.

Dedication

To the brave young men of the British and Allied forces who landed on the beaches of Normandy and to all those who never returned. Your courage and sacrifice gave us the freedom we cherish today. Unknowingly, you began a journey that continues in every generation, a journey toward recognising and protecting the dignity and privacy of every individual. From your sacrifice came the European Convention on Human Rights and, in time, the laws that safeguard our right to a private life.

And to my wife Caroline, for your love, patience, and unwavering support, you are my strength and my compass.

To our wonderful daughters Stephanie, Aimee, Elisha, and Georgina, whose curiosity, kindness, and love for life inspire me every day. To Max, for the joy and laughter you bring.

And to God, for His love, guidance, and the gift of all those who have made this journey so meaningful.

Acknowledgments

This book is the result of a lifetime of experiences, lessons, and the incredible people who have influenced and supported me along the way. I want to thank all those who saw potential in me and gave me the chance to grow, both personally and professionally.

To Mike Ormsby, thank you for giving me my big break at J.J. Fox and for trusting me to take on opportunities that shaped my early career. To Stan Cruickshank, your wisdom, patience, and guidance helped me see the value of professionalism and perseverance.

To all the dedicated police officers I had the privilege to work alongside during my 22 years with the States of Jersey Police, some good, some not so good, each of you taught me something important about life, leadership, and myself.

To Dr. Helen Miles, thank you for recognising and supporting my passion for change, and for your guidance when I took the leap to start my own business.

To the Propelfwd team, both past and present, your hard work, professionalism, and belief in what we do have built the company into the largest and most respected data protection consultancy in the Channel Islands. I am proud of all we've achieved together.

And finally and most importantly to my wife Caroline, for your endless love, support, and encouragement. You have been my constant motivation and the reason I strive to be a better person every day. To our beautiful daughters, Stephanie, Aimee, Elisha, and Georgina, you inspire me with your curiosity, kindness, and love for life and learning. To Max, the best dog anyone could ask for, thank you for the joy you bring into our home.

About the Author

Paul Byrne LL.M was born in Dublin, Ireland in 1968 and raised by his adoptive parents. Leaving full-time education at the age of fifteen, he began his career as a bar apprentice at a hotel in Kilternan, County Dublin. When the hotel closed in early 1985, Paul travelled to Jersey in the Channel Islands for what was meant to be a single summer season in hospitality, a move that would shape the rest of his life.

After a short time in the hospitality sector, Paul joined the tobacco importer J.J. Fox, where his talent for communication and organisation led to promotion as a sales executive. In 1995, seeking new challenges and a career with public purpose, Paul joined the States of Jersey Police, serving the community for 22 years and retiring in 2017 at the rank of Sergeant.

Following his retirement from policing, Paul channelled his experience in governance, investigation, and leadership into a new venture. He founded Propelfwd, a Jersey-based data protection consultancy dedicated to helping organisations turn complex data protection laws into practical, workable compliance.

Paul went on to earn a Master of Laws Degree (LL.M) in Information Rights Law and Practice, deepening his expertise in privacy and data governance. Today, he works with businesses, charities, and public bodies across the Channel Islands and the UK, guiding them to embed data protection principles into their daily operations.

Through his consultancy, teaching, and writing, Paul is recognised for making data protection understandable and achievable for everyone, helping organisations build trust, accountability, and respect into how they handle personal information.

When not working with clients or writing about data protection, Paul enjoys cycling and walking around Jersey's coastline with his wife Caroline and their dog, Max.

Acronym Key

AI – Artificial Intelligence

Computer systems designed to perform tasks that normally require human intelligence, such as decision-making, pattern recognition and natural language processing.

BCC – Blind Carbon Copy

An email function that hides recipients' addresses from others receiving the same message; relevant in data protection to prevent unintended disclosure.

CRM – Customer Relationship Management

A system used to manage interactions with customers and donors, often holding large volumes of personal data.

CTT – Cross-Border Transfer Tool

A general term for mechanisms (such as SCCs or IDTAs) that make international data transfers lawful.

DPA 2018 – Data Protection Act 2018

The UK's national law that supplements the UK GDPR, setting out additional rules, exemptions and enforcement powers.

DPIA – Data Protection Impact Assessment

A structured risk assessment required for high-risk processing under Article 35 GDPR, designed to identify and mitigate privacy risks.

DPGL – Data Protection (Bailiwick of Guernsey) Law 2017

The primary data protection law in Guernsey, aligned closely with GDPR principles.

DPJL – Data Protection (Jersey) Law 2018

The main data protection legislation in Jersey, based on the GDPR framework.

DPF – Data Privacy Framework

The current framework (2023) governing data transfers between the EU and US, replacing the invalidated Privacy Shield.

DUAA – Data (Use and Access) Act 2025

A UK law reforming certain aspects of the UK GDPR to simplify compliance and support innovation while maintaining safeguards.

EU GDPR – General Data Protection Regulation (Regulation (EU) 2016/679)

The core EU regulation governing personal data processing and protection across the European Economic Area (EEA).

ICO – Information Commissioner's Office

The UK's independent data protection authority responsible for enforcing the DPA 2018 and UK GDPR.

IDTA – International Data Transfer Agreement

The UK's contractual mechanism for lawful transfers of personal data to countries without adequacy decisions, similar to the EU's SCCs.

JOIC – Jersey Office of the Information Commissioner

Jersey's independent data protection regulator responsible for overseeing compliance with the DPJL.

ODPA – Office of the Data Protection Authority

Guernsey's data protection regulator responsible for enforcing the DPGL.

PECR – Privacy and Electronic Communications (EC Directive) Regulations 2003

UK regulations governing electronic marketing, cookies and other communications privacy issues.

ROPA – Record of Processing Activities

A record under Article 30 GDPR setting out what personal data an organisation processes, why, how and where.

SaaS – Software as a Service

Cloud-based software accessed via the internet; common in data governance, e.g., YourDataSafe and CookieScan.

DSAR – Data Subject Access Request

A request made by an individual to access personal data held about them under Article 15 GDPR.

SCCs – Standard Contractual Clauses

Legal templates issued by the EU to safeguard data transfers to countries without adequacy status.

UK GDPR – United Kingdom General Data Protection Regulation

The UK's version of the GDPR retained in domestic law following Brexit, alongside the Data Protection Act 2018.

Other Commonly Used Terms

Adequacy Decision

A formal recognition by the European Commission or the UK Secretary of State that another country provides equivalent data protection standards.

Breach Log

An internal record of data breaches and near misses, whether or not reported to regulators.

Controller

An organisation or person that determines the purpose and means of processing personal data.

Processor

A person or organisation that processes personal data on behalf of a controller.

Special Category Data

Sensitive personal data requiring extra protection, including health, religion, ethnicity, political beliefs and biometric or genetic data.

Third Sector

Charities, voluntary bodies and not-for-profit organisations operating for public or community benefit.

Contents

Foreword

LLM PgDip (Law) PGCert (Law)
PGCHE FBCS FCMI FEPRI

I am honoured to have been invited to contribute this foreword. It is a privilege to endorse a work that not only demonstrates substantial legal and academic rigour but also advances practical understanding within a sector that is often underserved by traditional data-protection scholarship. To be asked to support this publication signifies both professional respect and a shared commitment to the responsible and lawful management of personal data. I am grateful for the opportunity to lend my voice to a text that will undoubtedly inform, equip, and guide organisations as they navigate their statutory obligations and ethical responsibilities within the information-rights landscape.

Data has become an essential organisational asset, central to strategy, service delivery, commercial operations, and public trust. This is particularly true for small businesses, charities, and community organisations, where data holdings often include sensitive personal information relating to customers, beneficiaries, staff, volunteers, and service users. In such contexts, the lawful, fair, and transparent management of personal data is not merely a statutory requirement but an indicator of institutional responsibility and ethical governance.

The legal frameworks governing information rights and data protection within the British Islands and the broader European regulatory landscape set out clear principles relating to accountability, lawfulness, purpose limitation, data minimisation, accuracy, storage limitation, integrity, and confidentiality. These principles are articulated through instruments including the General Data Protection Regulation, the Data Protection Act 2018, the Data Protection (Jersey) Law 2018, the Data Protection (Bailiwick of Guernsey) Law 2017, the Privacy and Electronic Communications Regulations, and, of increasing relevance, the UK Data Use and Access Act 2025. Together, they impose legal obligations on controllers and processors to ensure that personal data is handled in a manner that protects the rights and freedoms of individuals while supporting legitimate organisational aims.

Compliance with these duties is frequently perceived as complex and onerous, particularly by smaller organisations without specialist legal or technical resources. However, as this book demonstrates, proportionate compliance can deliver substantial operational and strategic benefits. The very reason we need this book is to bridge a gap between complex legislation and multiple sources of often conflicting guidance. Sound data governance enhances public confidence, evidences organisational maturity, mitigates risks arising from regulatory investigation or civil liability, and provides a structured foundation for lawful innovation and responsible processing.

I have known Paul Byrne for several years and have supported his development as a practitioner within the information-rights domain. His academic achievement in obtaining the Master of Laws in Information Rights Law and Practice reflects significant intellectual engagement with this field and informs the depth of analysis present within this work. The text demonstrates a clear understanding of both statutory obligations and their real-world application, combining practical tools with legal authority in a manner that is rarely achieved in this area.

This book meets a demonstrable need within the data-protection landscape. Existing resources often adopt either a high-level introductory approach that lacks legal precision or a highly technical format aimed at corporate compliance teams. In contrast, this work offers a structured, legally grounded guide accessible to organisations with limited administrative capacity. Its use of plain English, supported by explicit legal references, case studies, practical templates, and proportionate methodologies, ensures that readers may implement lawful processing practices with clarity and confidence.

I commend this publication as a valuable contribution to the discipline of information rights and data protection. It will serve not merely to support compliance but to embed lawful and ethical data practices as an integral aspect of organisational governance.

Preface

by Paul Byrne

LL.M, FIP

When I first started working with small businesses and charities on data protection, one thing became immediately apparent: most of them were overwhelmed. They cared about doing the right thing, but they didn't know where to start. They heard "GDPR" and imagined mountains of paperwork, endless consent forms and threats of million-pound fines. Many felt paralysed.

At the same time, I saw the other side of the coin. Organisations that took even small, practical steps towards compliance quickly found unexpected benefits. They became more organised, more confident and more trusted by their customers, staff and donors. What initially appeared to be a burden often turned out to be an opportunity.

But I also noticed a gap. The resources available were either too basic, oversimplified guides that glossed over the legal requirements or too complex, written in dense legal language aimed at corporate compliance teams. Small organisations needed something different: a clear, practical handbook that spoke their language while still grounding everything in the law.

That is what this book sets out to provide. It takes the core legal frameworks, GDPR, the UK Data Protection Act, the Channel Islands' laws, PECR and the new Data (Use and Access) Act 2025 and explains them in plain English. It offers templates, checklists and real-world examples that small teams can adapt straight away. It also includes call-out boxes that show exactly where each requirement comes from in law, so you can be confident you're following the rules.

Most importantly, this book is written with empathy for the reality of small organisations. I know you are stretched. I know compliance is just one of many competing demands. That's why the guidance here is designed to be proportionate, achievable and useful, not just legally correct, but practical in everyday operations.

I hope this book not only helps you avoid mistakes but also empowers you to use data protection as a strength. Whether you are a small business building customer trust, a charity protecting your donors and service users, or a community organisation safeguarding children and volunteers, this book is for you.

Thank you for trusting me to be part of your compliance journey. I hope you will keep this book on your desk, mark it up and return to it whenever a new question arises. Data protection is not a one-off project; it is an ongoing commitment. However, with the right tools and guidance, it is a commitment that every organisation, regardless of its size, can meet with confidence.

Introduction: How to Use This Book

This book has been written for small businesses, charities and community organisations that want to get data protection right without getting bogged down in legal jargon. If you've ever wondered whether GDPR really applies to you, struggled with subject access requests, or worried about whether your website cookies are compliant, this book is for you.

What This Book Is

It is a practical handbook. You will not find dense legal analysis or pages of unexplained regulations. Instead, you will find plain-English explanations of what the law requires, alongside case studies, checklists and templates you can adapt to your own organisation.

At the same time, this is not a "lightweight" guide. Wherever the law matters, we reference it directly. Call-Out Boxes in each chapter highlight the specific articles of GDPR, the Data Protection (Jersey) Law 2018, the Data Protection (Bailiwick of Guernsey) Law 2017, the UK Data Protection Act 2018, PECR and the new Data (Use and Access) Act 2025. This means you can see precisely where each requirement comes from, without having to wade through the legislation yourself.

How to Use It

The book is structured in a way that allows you to either read it cover to cover or dip in and out as you need.

- **Part 1: Understanding the Foundations** introduces the laws, principles and context. If you are entirely new to data protection, start here.

- **Part 2: Practical Steps to Compliance** provides a step-by-step roadmap, guiding you through mapping your data, selecting lawful bases, managing rights and securing information.
- **Part 3: Applying Compliance to Common Scenarios** focuses on specific issues you are likely to face, such as marketing, working with third parties, special category data and children's data.
- **Part 4: Building a Culture of Compliance** helps you embed data protection into daily practice, including when and how to conduct DPIAs and whether you need a DPO.
- **Part 5: Resources and Tools** provide templates, checklists and references that you can use immediately.

You can follow the whole journey or skip directly to the sections most relevant to your current challenges. For example, if you are about to launch a new website, you may want to start by setting up cookies and implementing marketing strategies. If you are dealing with a subject access request, go directly to the chapter on individuals' rights.

A Proportionate Approach

Throughout this book, we emphasise proportionality. Regulators understand that a local café, a community charity, or a small retailer cannot implement the same measures as a global bank. The law allows you to scale compliance according to your size and resources, but it still expects you to comply.

Building Confidence

Finally, remember this: data protection is not about fear. It is about trust. By following the steps in this book, you will not only meet your legal obligations but also strengthen your organisation. You will build confidence with your customers, donors, volunteers and staff. You will make your operations more efficient. And you will know that you are doing the right thing by the people whose data you hold.

So, whether you are a business owner, a charity trustee, a manager, or simply the person in your organisation who has been asked to "sort out data protection," this book is here to guide you. Keep it on your desk, refer to it when questions arise and use the checklists and templates to put compliance into practice.

Part 1 - Understanding the Foundations

Introduces the laws, principles and context. If you are a novice when it comes to data protection, start here.

What You'll Learn

In this opening part, readers will understand why data protection matters, where the laws come from and how the core principles shape every decision. By the end of Part 1, you'll be able to explain the purpose of data protection, identify the key legal frameworks that apply to your organisation and describe the seven fundamental principles in plain English.

Chapter 1: Why Data Protection Matters for Small Organisations

Explores why good data protection builds trust, prevents reputational damage and improves efficiency. It explains the real risks of non-compliance for small enterprises and charities and how getting it right strengthens relationships and confidence.

Chapter 2: The Legal Landscape

Sets out the GDPR, UK GDPR and Channel Islands laws, how they fit together and where the DUAA and PECR sit in the picture. It helps readers see the bigger framework and identify which rules apply to them.

Chapter 3: The Principles of Data Protection – The Backbone of Compliance

Breaks down the seven GDPR principles with practical, relatable examples showing how they operate in everyday decisions and record-keeping.

Chapter 1: Why Data Protection Matters for Small Organisations

Many small businesses and third-sector organisations view data protection as something designed for large corporations, with teams of lawyers and compliance officers. But the reality is that every organisation, no matter how small, handles personal data. Whether it's customer records, volunteer contact details, donor information, or staff files, you are responsible for treating that information properly.

The importance of data protection cannot be overstated. It's not just about avoiding fines or ticking a regulatory box. It's about trust, reputation, efficiency and doing the right thing by the people whose information you hold. In this chapter, we'll explore why data protection matters, the risks of ignoring it, the benefits of compliance and the common myths that often hold smaller organisations back.

Risks of Non-Compliance

When most people think of data protection risks, they imagine huge fines splashed across the news. And yes, fines are a real possibility. The GDPR, the UK GDPR and the Channel Islands' laws allow regulators to issue penalties of up to €20 million or 4% of annual global turnover, whichever is higher. Even though small organisations are unlikely to face the maximum, regulators can and do fine charities, schools, local clubs and SMEs when things go wrong.

For example, in the UK, a small pharmacy was fined £275,000 for leaving patient records unsecured. In Jersey, the JOIC has reprimanded charities for failing to respond properly to subject access requests. These are not abstract risks; they affect organisations with limited resources and tight budgets.

But fines are not the only concern. Non-compliance brings several other risks:

- **Reputational damage:** A single data breach can erode years of trust. A charity that leaks donor information may find supporters withdrawing, while a café that mishandles customer loyalty data might see negative reviews and reduced footfall.
- **Loss of business opportunities:** Increasingly, customers, partners and funders ask about your data protection practices. If you can't demonstrate compliance, you may miss out on contracts or grants.
- **Operational disruption:** Dealing with a data breach, subject access request, or regulatory investigation can absorb enormous amounts of time. For small teams, this distraction can halt normal operations.
- **Personal liability:** In some jurisdictions, including the Channel Islands, directors and trustees can be held personally responsible if an organisation seriously breaches data protection law.

📌 **Call-Out Box: The Legal Foundation for Risks**

The powers to fine, investigate and issue enforcement notices come from Articles 58 and 83 of the GDPR. These provisions are mirrored in the Data Protection Authority (Jersey) Law 2018, Part 4 and the Data Protection (Bailiwick of Guernsey) Law 2017, Part XI & XII. Regulators in the UK (ICO), Jersey (JOIC) and Guernsey (ODPA) all actively use these powers.

Benefits of Compliance

It is easy to think of compliance as a burden. But there are significant benefits when data protection is done properly.

First and foremost, it builds trust. Donors, customers, employees and volunteers all want to feel confident that their information is in safe hands. If you can demonstrate that you are careful, transparent and responsible, you set yourself apart from less diligent organisations.

Second, compliance creates efficiency. Data mapping and good governance might seem like paperwork, but they often highlight duplication, outdated systems and unnecessary information. A charity that discovers it is storing old volunteer records across three systems can streamline its processes and save money. A small business that sets clear retention rules will avoid drowning in irrelevant files.

Third, compliance gives you confidence in decision-making. If you know exactly what data you hold, where it is and why you use it, you are better placed to respond to new opportunities. Want to launch an email newsletter? You'll know which customers have given valid consent. Considering moving to a new SaaS platform? You'll know what security and contractual terms you need.

Finally, compliance helps with resilience and risk management. Organisations that take data protection seriously are better prepared for cyberattacks, system failures, or accidental losses. Having a breach response plan in place means you can act quickly and reduce harm if something does go wrong.

Common Misconceptions Among Small Organisations

One reason small organisations hesitate to engage with data protection is because of persistent myths. Let's tackle the most common ones.

"We're too small for GDPR to apply to us."

This is false. The law applies to *any organisation* that processes personal data, regardless of size. What changes is how you comply. The law allows for a proportionate approach, so your compliance framework should be appropriate to your scale and resources, but it must still exist.

"We don't handle personal data."

Most organisations do, often without realising it. If you hold names, phone numbers, email addresses, photographs, donation histories, or even IP addresses, you are processing personal data. Even a local sports club with a list of members' names and contact details falls under data protection law.

"Data protection is just about consent."

Consent is only one of several lawful bases for processing data. In fact, many small organisations rely more on contract or legitimate interests. Understanding the full range of lawful bases makes compliance much easier and reduces unnecessary reliance on consent forms.

"It's all just red tape."

While there are formal requirements, much of compliance is about common sense. Being clear about why you collect data, keeping it secure and not holding onto it forever are not exotic requirements; they are simply good practice.

"We'll never be fined."

It's true that regulators target larger organisations as they should be more accountable for their data protection practices. But they regularly investigate and reprimand smaller ones. Even if you are not fined, the disruption and reputational damage from a regulatory investigation can be severe.

> ★ **Call-Out Box: Proportionality in Law**
>
> Recital 13 of the GDPR makes clear that small organisations are not exempt from the regulation, but that compliance measures should be proportionate to the nature, scope, context and purposes of processing. This proportionality is also built into the Channel Islands' laws. It means that you can scale your approach to fit your organisation, but you cannot ignore the law altogether.

Case Studies: Lessons Learned

To make this real, let's look at a few examples.

Case Study 1: The Small Retailer

A boutique café collected customer emails for a loyalty scheme but never set up a proper unsubscribe mechanism. A complaint to the ICO led to an investigation. While the café was not fined, it was ordered to stop its practices immediately and invest in compliance training. The owner admitted that the reputational impact, negative press and angry customers were worse than any fine.

Case Study 2: The Local Charity

A community charity failed to respond to a data subject access request from a former volunteer. The JOIC reprimanded the charity, requiring new processes and policies. The trustee board had to spend months reviewing governance documents. Donors became aware of the incident and the charity had to work hard to rebuild trust.

Case Study 3: The Small School

A small independent school suffered a ransomware attack that exposed parents' and pupils' data. Although the school notified the ODPA and acted quickly, it faced a regulatory investigation and had to invest heavily in new IT systems. The breach highlighted the risks of outdated security and inadequate contingency planning.

Conclusion

Data protection matters for every organisation, no matter how small. The risks of non-compliance include fines, reputational harm, lost opportunities and disruption. The benefits of compliance include trust, efficiency, resilience and confidence. And the common myths that small organisations are exempt, that it's all about consent, or that only large firms need to worry are just that: myths.

By taking data protection seriously, you not only stay on the right side of the law but also strengthen your organisation. The rest of this book will show you how to do that in a proportionate, practical way that supports your mission rather than distracting from it.

By the way, the case studies are not real events, just examples to get your brain thinking about what you do in your organisation and if the example given could be you?

📌 **Call-Out Box: Key Legal References from this Chapter**

- Article 5 GDPR: Principles of data protection (accountability, fairness, minimisation, etc.)
- Article 6 GDPR: Lawful bases for processing personal data
- Articles 58 & 83 GDPR: Regulatory powers, including fines and investigations
- Recital 13 GDPR: Proportionality for small organisations
- DPJL (Jersey) and DPGL (Guernsey): Local equivalents of GDPR, aligned with the same principles
- DUAA: Introduces recognised legitimate interests and

Chapter 2: The Legal Landscape

When people hear "data protection law," they often imagine a single set of rules. In reality, organisations in the UK and Channel Islands operate under a patchwork of overlapping frameworks. The good news is that they share common foundations, so if you understand the principles behind one, you are most of the way towards compliance with the others.

This chapter will guide you through the main laws you need to know about: the EU GDPR, the UK GDPR and the Data Protection Act 2018, the Channel Islands' data protection laws and the related frameworks that apply to electronic marketing and cookies (PECR and the ePrivacy Directive). We'll also look at the new Data (Use and Access) Act 2025, which introduces some important updates.

By the end of this chapter, you should understand how these laws fit together, why they exist and how they affect your organisation.

The General Data Protection Regulation (GDPR)

The General Data Protection Regulation (GDPR) came into force in May 2018 across the European Union. It replaced older patchwork national laws with a single, harmonised framework. Its goals were simple but ambitious: to strengthen individuals' rights, create consistency across the EU and increase accountability for organisations handling personal data.

GDPR applies to any organisation that processes the data of people in the EU, even if that organisation is outside the EU. This "extra-territorial" reach means that if a Jersey charity runs a fundraising campaign targeting French residents, or a UK business sells products to German customers, they must comply with GDPR.

Key features of GDPR include:

- Stronger rights for individuals, including the right to access, rectify, erase and restrict their data.
- Stricter rules on transparency, requiring clear and accessible privacy notices.
- A requirement for organisations to demonstrate accountability through records, policies and governance.
- Heavy penalties for breaches, with fines of up to €20 million or 4% of global turnover.

Although it is often portrayed as a bureaucratic burden, GDPR is designed to be flexible. Recital 13 explicitly states that small organisations can take a proportionate approach. That does not mean exemptions, it means you scale your compliance measures to your size, resources and risk profile.

> 📌 **Call-Out Box: Legal Reference**
>
> GDPR Articles 1–3: Establish the regulation's scope and extra-territorial effect.
>
> GDPR Articles 12–22: Individuals' rights.
>
> GDPR Article 30: Records of processing activities (ROPA).
>
> GDPR Articles 58 & 83: Enforcement powers and fines.

The UK GDPR and Data Protection Act 2018

When the UK left the EU, it retained GDPR in domestic law. The result is the UK GDPR, which sits alongside the Data Protection Act 2018 (DPA 2018).

For most small organisations, the differences between EU GDPR and UK GDPR are minimal. The core principles, lawful bases and rights are identical. Where you need to be alert is if you are processing data across borders. If you offer goods or services to EU residents, you may have to comply with both regimes. In practice, this often means maintaining compliance with EU GDPR to ensure free data flows.

The Data Protection Act 2018 supplements the UK GDPR. It fills in areas where GDPR left room for national rules, such as exemptions for journalism, research, law enforcement and national security processing. It also sets out the role and powers of the UK Information Commissioner's Office (ICO).

📌 **Call-Out Box: Legal Reference**

- UK GDPR: Largely mirrors the EU GDPR but applies domestically.

- Data Protection Act 2018, Part 2: Supplements GDPR with UK-specific exemptions and rules.

- DPA 2018, Schedule 1: Conditions for processing special category and criminal offence data.

Channel Islands Data Protection Laws

Both the Bailiwick of Jersey and the Bailiwick of Guernsey have their own data protection frameworks. These are designed to be equivalent to GDPR so that data can flow freely between the islands, the UK and the EU.

- Jersey: Data Protection (Jersey) Law 2018 (DPJL)
- Guernsey: Data Protection (Bailiwick of Guernsey) Law 2017 (DPGL)

The structures mirror GDPR closely: the same principles, rights and obligations apply. The local regulators, the JOIC in Jersey and the ODPA in Guernsey, enforce compliance. Both authorities emphasise a proportionate, supportive approach to smaller organisations, but they have shown they are willing to take enforcement action where necessary.

One difference is that both island laws include explicit recognition of the human right to privacy under local human rights legislation. They also reflect the islands' status as "adequate" jurisdictions, meaning the EU recognises them as offering GDPR-level protection.

📌 **Call-Out Box: Legal Reference**

- DPJL, Part 2: Fundamental Duties of Controllers.

- DPJL, Part 6: Rights of individuals.

- DPGL, Parts 2–3: Equivalent provisions in Guernsey.

- Human Rights (Jersey) Law 2000 and Human Rights (Bailiwick of Guernsey) Law 2000: Privacy as a fundamental right.

PECR and the ePrivacy Directive

GDPR is not the only relevant law. If your organisation uses email, SMS, or cookies for marketing, you must also comply with the Privacy and Electronic Communications Regulations 2003 (PECR) in the UK, or the ePrivacy Directive in the EU.

These rules cover:

- Direct marketing: When you can send marketing emails, texts, or phone calls and when you need consent.
- Cookies and similar technologies: The need for consent before setting non-essential cookies (such as analytics or tracking cookies).
- Electronic communications security: Rules around confidentiality of communications and preventing interception.

PECR is often where small organisations trip up. Sending fundraising emails without proper consent or using a cookie banner that doesn't actually block cookies until consent is given are common pitfalls.

The upcoming ePrivacy Regulation is expected to replace the current Directive, but at the time of writing, it has not yet been finalised.

> 📌 **Call-Out Box: Legal Reference**
>
> - PECR Regulation 22: Direct marketing by electronic mail.
> - PECR Regulation 6: Use of cookies and similar technologies.
> - ePrivacy Directive, Article 5(3): Consent requirement for cookies.

The Data (Use and Access) Act 2025

The most recent development in the UK is the Data (Use and Access) Act 2025 (DUAA), which received Royal Assent in June 2025. This Act does not replace GDPR or PECR, but it makes some important changes.

Key updates include:

- Recognised legitimate interests: The Act introduces a list of activities that can be assumed to be legitimate interests without requiring a balancing test. These include internal record-keeping, network security and some types of fundraising.
- Low-risk storage and access technologies: The Act allows for limited use of low-risk technologies, including some cookies, without explicit consent.
- Digital verification and smart data frameworks: New provisions support innovation in areas like identity verification and consumer data portability.

📌 **Call-Out Box: Legal Reference**

- DUAA, Part 2: Recognised legitimate interests.

- DUAA, Part 3: Low-risk storage and access technologies.

- ICO Guidance (2025): Explains how DUAA interacts with UK GDPR and PECR.

For small organisations, the DUAA offers some welcome simplifications. For example, charities sending postal fundraising letters may now be able to rely on recognised legitimate interests more confidently. However, the ICO has emphasised that this does not remove the need for fairness, transparency, or safeguards.

How These Laws Fit Together

It can feel overwhelming to juggle multiple laws, but the reality is simpler than it seems. Think of GDPR (or its local equivalent) as the foundation, it sets the principles, lawful bases, rights and obligations. Then layer on:

- The UK Data Protection Act 2018, which supplements GDPR in the UK.
- The Channel Islands laws, which mirror GDPR locally.
- PECR/ePrivacy, which covers direct marketing and cookies.
- The DUAA, which tweaks and clarifies some aspects, particularly around legitimate interests and cookies.

As a small organisation, if you build your compliance programme around the GDPR principles, with attention to PECR for your marketing and cookies, you will cover 95% of your obligations. The DUAA and local Channel Islands laws introduce some nuances, but they do not change the fundamentals.

Case Studies: Navigating the Legal Landscape

Case Study 1: A UK SME Selling to France

A small online retailer in the UK sells goods to customers in France. Even though it operates from the UK, it must comply with both UK GDPR and EU GDPR because it is targeting EU residents. It also needs to follow PECR rules for email marketing. By basing its practices on GDPR principles, it can meet both sets of obligations.

Case Study 2: A Jersey Charity Fundraising Online

A Jersey-based charity runs a fundraising campaign using email and social media. It must comply with the DPJL, but because it is targeting donors in France, the EU GDPR also applies. It must also consider ePrivacy rules if it sends electronic communications. By using CookieScan to manage its cookie consent, it ensures compliance with both PECR and ePrivacy.

Case Study 3: A Guernsey Tech Start-up Using Cookies

A Guernsey start-up develops a website that uses analytics cookies. Under DPGL and PECR, it must obtain consent before setting those cookies. Under DUAA, it may benefit from some flexibility for low-risk technologies, but it still needs to ensure transparency and fairness. Using CookieScan ensures the cookie banner meets the legal standard.

Conclusion

The data protection legal landscape may appear complex, but the core principles are consistent across frameworks. GDPR, UK GDPR, the Channel Islands' laws, PECR, ePrivacy and the DUAA all share the same goal: to protect individuals' personal data and ensure organisations use it responsibly.

For small organisations, the key is not to get lost in the technicalities. Focus on the principles, be transparent, secure your data and apply proportionate measures. With that foundation, you will not only comply with the law but also build trust with the people who matter most, your customers, donors, volunteers and staff.

Remember, the case studies are not real events, just examples to get your brain thinking about what you do in your organisation and if the example given could be you?

📌 **Call-Out Box: Key Legal References from this Chapter**

- GDPR Articles 1–3, 12–22, 30, 58 & 83

- UK GDPR + Data Protection Act 2018 (Part 2, Schedule 1)

- DPJL and DPGL

- PECR Regulations 6 & 22 / ePrivacy Directive Article 5(3)

- DUAA, Parts 2 & 3

Chapter 3: The Principles of Data Protection – The Backbone of Compliance

At the heart of all data protection laws lie a set of principles. These principles are not optional extras. They are the foundation upon which every compliance requirement is built. If you understand and apply these principles, you will find that many of the detailed rules start to make sense.

The General Data Protection Regulation (GDPR) sets out seven key principles in Article 5. The UK GDPR, the Data Protection (Jersey) Law 2018 (DPJL) and the Data Protection (Bailiwick of Guernsey) Law 2017 (DPGL) all mirror these principles. Regulators like the ICO, JOIC and ODPA consistently refer back to them when investigating complaints or deciding on enforcement action.

This chapter will unpack each principle in turn, show how it applies in practice for small organisations and provide examples of how to embed them in day-to-day operations.

Principle 1: Lawfulness, Fairness and Transparency

You must process personal data lawfully, fairly and in a way that is transparent to individuals.

- **Lawfulness** means you must have a valid lawful basis for processing (from Article 6 GDPR). For special category data, you also need an Article 9 condition.

- **Fairness** means you don't mislead people or use their data in unexpected or harmful ways.
- **Transparency** means being open and clear through privacy notices, policies and honest communication.

Example:

A small community centre collects parents' details when children join an after-school club. If the centre explains why it is collecting the data, how long it will keep it and who it may share it with, it is meeting transparency requirements. If it later sold those details to a marketing company, that would breach fairness and lawfulness.

📌 **Call-Out Box: Legal Reference**

- GDPR Article 5(1)(a): Lawfulness, fairness, transparency.
- GDPR Article 6: Lawful bases.
- DPJL, Part 2 / DPGL, Part 2: Mirror provisions.

Principle 2: Purpose Limitation

You must only collect personal data for specified, explicit and legitimate purposes and you cannot use it for a completely different purpose later.

Example:

A charity collects contact details from people who sign up to a sponsored walk, so it can manage the event. Using those details later to send marketing about unrelated fundraising without informing them first would breach the purpose limitation.

In practice, this means being clear at the point of collection about why you want the data and not straying too far from that purpose unless you have a lawful reason.

Principle 3: Data Minimisation

You must ensure that personal data is adequate, relevant and limited to what is necessary for the purpose.

Example:

If a local gym signs up new members, it needs their name, contact details and payment information; asking for marital status, ethnicity, or next of kin without a specific need would breach data minimisation.

Minimisation prevents "just in case" collection. For small organisations, this helps keep records lean and reduces risk.

Principle 4: Accuracy

Personal data must be accurate and kept up to date. Inaccurate data should be corrected or deleted without delay.

Example:
A charity maintains a donor mailing list. If a donor moves house but continues to receive letters at their old address, this is inaccurate and risks breaching accuracy requirements. Not only does it waste resources, but it also risks reputational harm if letters are delivered to the wrong person.

Organisations should put in place simple processes for people to update their details and should review records periodically.

> 📌 **Call-Out Box: Legal Reference**
>
> • GDPR Article 5(1)(d): Accuracy.
>
> • GDPR Article 16: Right to rectification.

Principle 5: Storage Limitation

Personal data should not be kept longer than necessary. Once it has served its purpose, it should be securely deleted or anonymised.

Example:
A local theatre holds volunteer application forms. It decides to keep them indefinitely in case the volunteers return. This is a breach. Instead, it should set a retention period, perhaps two years for unsuccessful applications and a limited period after a volunteer leaves.

Retention schedules help manage this. Even a simple table that sets out how long to keep staff records, donor records and customer data can go a long way.

Principle 6: Integrity and Confidentiality (Security)

You must keep personal data secure, using appropriate technical and organisational measures. This includes protecting against unauthorised access, accidental loss, or destruction.

Example:
A local café keeps its staff rota on an open spreadsheet accessible via a shared link. Because it includes staff phone numbers and shift patterns, this creates risks of unauthorised access. A better practice would be to use a secure, password-protected system with restricted access.

Security measures should be proportionate. For some organisations, this means strong passwords and staff training. For others, it may involve encryption, two-factor authentication and regular audits.

Principle 7: Accountability

The final principle underpins all the others: organisations must not only comply but also be able to demonstrate compliance.

This is where records of processing, policies, staff training and governance frameworks come in. Accountability means you can show your working if challenged.

Example:

If a donor asks how their data is used, a charity with a clear privacy notice, a data inventory and a retention schedule can respond quickly. A charity with no records or policies will struggle to prove compliance.

Accountability is also where tools like YourDataSafe help. By keeping records, requests and breaches in one place, you create an audit trail that demonstrates compliance.

How the Principles Work Together

Although listed separately, these principles reinforce each other. Transparency supports fairness. Minimisation reduces security risks. Accountability ties everything together.

For small organisations, the key is to treat the principles as a checklist for every new activity. If you are starting a new project, ask:

- Are we being transparent?
- Do we have a lawful basis?
- Are we collecting only what we need?
- Will the data be accurate and up to date?
- Do we know how long we'll keep it?
- Have we secured it properly?
- Can we show we've thought it through?

If the answer is yes to all of these, you are well on your way to compliance.

Case Studies: Principles in Action

Case Study 1: The Membership Club

A small sports club collects names, addresses and contact details for members. It clearly explains this in a privacy notice (transparency), uses the details only for managing memberships (purpose limitation) and keeps them in a secure online system (security). When members leave, it deletes their data after two years (storage limitation). The club keeps a simple record of all this (accountability).

Case Study 2: The Food Bank

A local food bank collects information about clients, including names, addresses and household details. Because it sometimes handles sensitive data (health or financial circumstances), it applies extra safeguards (lawfulness and fairness). It minimises collection by asking only what is necessary to provide support. It ensures accuracy by checking details regularly and it deletes records after three years (storage limitation).

Case Study 3: The SME Retailer

A small retailer uses a cloud-based CRM. It ensures the supplier offers strong security (integrity and confidentiality), keeps only relevant customer information (minimisation) and allows customers to update details online (accuracy). It keeps a ROPA in YourDataSafe (accountability).

Conclusion

The seven principles of data protection are the backbone of compliance. They are simple to understand but powerful in practice. For small organisations, applying these principles proportionately means you can avoid most compliance risks, build trust with your stakeholders and demonstrate responsibility.

If you use these principles as your constant guide, your "north star," every decision about personal data will be easier.

📌 **Call-Out Box: Key Legal References from this Chapter**

- GDPR Article 5(1)(a–f) & 5(2): The seven principles + accountability.

- GDPR Articles 6, 9, 16, 30, 32: Supporting obligations.

- DPJL (Part 2) / DPGL (Part 2): Channel Islands equivalents.

- DUAA: Adjusts accountability and legitimate interest's considerations.

Part 2 - Practical Steps to Compliance

A step-by-step roadmap: mapping your data, choosing lawful bases, managing rights and securing information.

What You'll Learn

This part turns principles into action. You'll learn how to map and understand your data, select lawful bases, document accountability, manage individual rights requests and protect information through proportionate security. By the end, you'll have a clear picture of what compliance looks like in daily operations.

Chapter 4: Know Your Data

Shows you how to identify and document what personal data you hold, where it flows and who has access. Introduces practical mapping techniques and the Record of Processing Activities (ROPA).

Chapter 5: Lawful Bases for Processing

Explains each lawful basis under Articles 6 and 9 GDPR, when to use them and how to record decisions so your processing is transparent and justified.

Chapter 6: Accountability in Practice

Describes how to evidence compliance through governance, policies, logs and review cycles. Helps you demonstrate that "we comply" with proof, not assumption.

Chapter 7: Individuals' Rights Made Practical

Translates subject-rights obligations into step-by-step processes for small organisations. Covers access, rectification, erasure and objection, with realistic response timelines.

Chapter 8: Data Security and Breach Management

Guides you through risk-based security, recognising and reporting breaches and maintaining breach logs so lessons are learned and regulators see accountability.

Chapter 4: Know Your Data

If there is one step that underpins every other part of data protection compliance, it is understanding what data you hold, why you hold it and how you use it. Without this knowledge, you cannot choose the right lawful basis, write accurate privacy notices, respond properly to subject access requests, or manage data securely.

Think of it as building a map. Just as you wouldn't set out on a journey without knowing the terrain, you can't build a compliance framework without knowing your data landscape. For small organisations, this can feel daunting, but it doesn't need to be. With the right approach and sometimes with the help of the right tools, you can create a manageable and effective record of your data.

Why Data Mapping Matters

Data mapping is the process of identifying the personal data you collect, where it is stored, who you share it with and how long you keep it. This information is then recorded in a data inventory.

For some organisations, this takes the form of a Record of Processing Activities (ROPA). Article 30 GDPR requires organisations with 250 or more employees or those engaged in high-risk or regular processing to maintain such a record. Even if you are smaller and not strictly obliged, regulators in the UK, Jersey and Guernsey all recommend keeping at least a basic version. It is the simplest way to demonstrate accountability.

The benefits go beyond compliance. A good data inventory helps you to:

- Identify unnecessary data collection ("Do we really need this?").
- Spot security risks (like sensitive data stored in spreadsheets).

- Make retention decisions (knowing what can be deleted saves time and money).
- Respond to subject access requests quickly.
- Show regulators, partners, or funders that you are responsible and organised.

> 📌 **Call-Out Box: Legal Reference**
>
> - GDPR Article 30: Record of processing activities.
>
> - Recital 13 GDPR: Proportionality - small organisations still expected to keep basic records.
>
> - DPJL, Article 14 / DPGL, Section 37: Jersey and Guernsey equivalents.

Getting Started with Data Inventories

The first step is to create a list of all the personal data your organisation holds. For each type, record:

- What the data is (e.g., names, addresses, health data).
- Why you collect it (the purpose).
- The lawful basis for processing (Article 6 GDPR and Article 9 if Special Category).
- Where it is stored (paper, local drives, cloud platforms).
- Who you share it with (suppliers, partners, regulators).
- How long you keep it (retention period).
- Any special risks (e.g., international transfers).

At its simplest, this can be done in a spreadsheet. But for organisations that want to save time and improve accuracy, compliance SaaS platforms like YourDataSafe offer a structured way to capture this information.

Using SaaS Tools to Support Governance

YourDataSafe is designed to make data protection governance easier for smaller organisations. It guides you step-by-step through creating your ROPA, prompting you for the information regulators expect. Because it is cloud-based, multiple team members can update records without duplicating spreadsheets.

Beyond the data inventory, YourDataSafe can also:

- Track and manage subject access requests (DSARs).
- Log and monitor data breaches.
- Store key policies and procedures.
- Generate compliance reports for trustees, boards, or regulators.

> 📌 **Call-Out Box: DUAA and Governance**
>
> The Data (Use and Access) Act 2025 simplifies some governance requirements for smaller organisations. It introduces recognised legitimate interests, which can be recorded in your ROPA without needing a balancing test. It also allows certain low-risk storage and access technologies (including some cookies) without explicit consent. Using a tool like CookieScan ensures you stay within the limits of these new rules.

For website compliance, CookieScan complements this work. It scans your website, identifies cookies and tracking technologies, categorises them and generates a compliant cookie banner. This ensures you meet your obligations under PECR and the ePrivacy Directive, while aligning with GDPR's transparency principle. Together, these tools reduce administrative effort and help smaller organisations demonstrate accountability in practice.

Worked Example: Data Inventory

Here is a simple example of a data inventory for a small business and a charity.

This table shows at a glance what, why and how of your data processing. Even a simple version like this can put you far ahead of many small organisations.

Use a Vertical Table (Stacked Format)

Instead of a wide spreadsheet, present each entry as a stacked record with short labels. For example:

Processing Activity: Customer contact details

Purpose: Manage sales orders and provide customer service

Lawful Basis: Contract (Art. 6(1)(b) GDPR)

Storage Location: Cloud CRM (EU server)

Sharing: Internal staff only

Retention: 6 years (aligned with the limitation period for contract claims)

Notes: Required under Art. 30 GDPR; demonstrates accountability

Processing Activity: Employee HR files (contracts, payroll, sickness records)

Purpose: Manage employment relationship

Lawful Basis: Legal obligation (Art. 6(1)(c) GDPR) + Special category (health) (Art. 9(2)(b) GDPR)

Storage Location: Encrypted HR SaaS platform (UK server)

Sharing: Payroll provider (UK)

Retention: Duration of employment + 6 years

Notes: DPA 2018 Schedule 1 sets additional conditions for processing employee health data

Processing Activity: Donor names and addresses

Purpose: Fundraising campaigns and donor communications

Lawful Basis: Legitimate interests (Art. 6(1)(f) GDPR) / Recognised legitimate interest (DUAA)

Storage Location: Secure cloud spreadsheet

Sharing: Mailing house (processor, under DPA)

Retention: 2 years after last donation

Notes: ICO confirms postal fundraising may rely on legitimate interests

Processing Activity: Website visitor data (cookies, analytics)

Purpose: Measure website traffic and improve services

Lawful Basis: Consent (Art. 6(1)(a) GDPR + PECR Reg 6) / Low-risk exemption (DUAA)

Storage Location: CookieScan platform
Sharing: Analytics provider (outside EU, SCCs in place)

Retention: 13 months

Notes: CookieScan helps ensure consent and transparency; PECR and ePrivacy still apply

Processing Activity: Safeguarding records (children's club attendance, incident reports)

Purpose: Ensure the safety and well-being of children

Lawful Basis: Legal obligation (Art. 6(1)(c) GDPR) + Special category (Art. 9(2)(g) GDPR – safeguarding)

Storage Location: Paper files in locked cabinet + scanned copies in secure cloud

Sharing: Safeguarding board, police if required

Retention: Until the child reaches age 25

Explaining a Spreadsheet-Based ROPA in Words

When you build a Record of Processing Activities (ROPA), the simplest tool is often a spreadsheet. Spreadsheets allow you to create clear columns for the main information you need to record and they make it easy to filter, sort and update entries.

Typically, you would create a spreadsheet with the following columns:

1. Data Category – what type of data it is (e.g., customer details, donor records, staff files).

2. Purpose – why you are collecting or using the data (e.g., managing sales, fundraising, payroll).

3. Lawful basis – the legal reason under GDPR or Channel Islands law (e.g., contract, legal obligation, legitimate interests).

4. Storage Location – where the data is kept (e.g., cloud CRM, paper file, HR system).

5. Sharing – who you share it with (e.g., suppliers, mailing houses, regulators).

6. Retention – how long you will keep it (e.g., 6 years, 2 years after last donation).

7. Notes – additional details, such as references to GDPR articles or risks.

For example, one row in your spreadsheet might read:

- Data Category: Customer details

- Purpose: Manage sales orders

- Lawful Basis: Contract (Art. 6(1)(b) GDPR)

- Storage Location: Cloud CRM (EU server)

- Sharing: Staff only

- Retention: 6 years

- Notes: Included in ROPA to show compliance with Art. 30 GDPR

Keeping It Up to Date

A data inventory is not a one-off exercise. It should be reviewed and updated when:

- You launch a new project or service.

- You start using a new system or supplier.

- You change how you collect or share data.

- You introduce or retire staff functions.

For small organisations, an annual review is usually sufficient unless something major changes. By using SaaS platforms like YourDataSafe, updates become part of routine governance rather than a burden.

⚠ A Word of Caution on Using Spreadsheets

Spreadsheets are often the first tool that small organisations reach for when building a data inventory or ROPA. They are familiar, low-cost and flexible. For many, they feel like the natural starting point. But relying solely on spreadsheets brings risks that you need to be aware of.

First, spreadsheets are prone to human error. A simple copy-and-paste mistake, or an accidental deletion, can change or wipe entire sections of your record. Without strong version control, it can be difficult to know which version is the most accurate. If several people are updating the same file, errors can creep in quickly.

Second, spreadsheets are not secure by default. If your ROPA spreadsheet contains sensitive details about staff, donors, or service users, storing it on a shared drive or emailing it between colleagues creates security vulnerabilities. Password protection on an Excel file is not the same as proper encryption and it is easily bypassed.

Third, spreadsheets don't scale well. As your organisation grows or your processing activities expand, the spreadsheet can become unwieldy. Dozens of rows, multiple tabs and inconsistent formatting can make it hard to maintain. Regulators expect you to be able to produce accurate records on request. An over-complicated spreadsheet can make that difficult.

Finally, spreadsheets lack audit trails. One of the key requirements under the accountability principle is being able to demonstrate compliance. Spreadsheets do not automatically track who made changes, when they were made, or why. If you are ever challenged by a regulator, you may struggle to prove that your records are reliable.

For these reasons, many organisations eventually move from spreadsheets to dedicated compliance tools. Platforms like YourDataSafe reduce the risk of error, improve security and provide clear audit trails. If you do start with a spreadsheet, treat it as a stepping stone rather than a permanent solution.

📌 **Call-Out Box: Accountability and Spreadsheets**

The accountability principle (Article 5(2) GDPR) requires organisations not only to comply with data protection rules but also to demonstrate compliance. While a spreadsheet may satisfy this requirement in the short term, it becomes harder to demonstrate accountability as your records grow more complex.

Case Studies: Mapping in Practice

Case Study 1: The Café Loyalty Scheme

A café runs a loyalty card programme. Initially, staff kept customer emails in a paper notebook. After creating a data inventory, the café realised this was insecure and inconsistent. They moved the list into a secure CRM, updated their privacy notice and limited access to the manager only.

Case Study 2: The Local Charity

A charity used to store volunteer details across personal laptops, emails and shared drives. By mapping its data, it identified the risk of duplication and loss. It centralised records in YourDataSafe, introduced retention periods and reassured trustees that risks were under control.

Case Study 3: The Community Website

A small community group used a website with analytics cookies but had no cookie banner. After scanning with CookieScan, they discovered multiple third-party cookies they hadn't known about. They implemented a compliant banner and updated their privacy notice.

Conclusion

Knowing your data is the foundation of compliance. A simple data inventory or full ROPA, if required, gives you clarity, reduces risk and supports every other part of your data protection journey. With proportionate effort, supported by tools like YourDataSafe and CookieScan, even the smallest organisations can demonstrate accountability and compliance.

In the next chapter, we'll build on this by exploring lawful bases for processing how to decide whether you need consent, when you can rely on the contract and how to apply legitimate interests fairly and safely.

📌 **Call-Out Box: Key Legal References from this Chapter**

- GDPR Article 30: Records of processing activities.

- GDPR Articles 6 & 9: Lawful bases and conditions for special category data.

- PECR Regulation 6 / ePrivacy Directive Art. 5(3): Cookies and consent.

- DUAA, Part 2 & 3: Recognised legitimate interests and low-risk technologies.

- DPJL / DPGL: Local equivalents.

Chapter 5: Lawful Bases for Processing

One of the most important questions you must answer in data protection compliance is: "What is our lawful basis for processing this personal data?"

The law requires every processing activity, whether collecting customer emails, storing employee records, or analysing website traffic, to have a lawful basis under Article 6 of the GDPR (or the equivalent in UK and Channel Islands law). For sensitive "special category" data, you also need an additional condition under Article 9.

Choosing the correct lawful basis is not just a box-ticking exercise. It determines how you communicate with individuals, how you handle rights requests and how regulators will judge your compliance. If you get it wrong, you risk undermining trust and breaching the law.

This chapter will explain the six lawful bases, when to use each, and how recent changes under the Data (Use and Access) Act 2025 (DUAA) affect organisations in practice.

The Six Lawful Bases under GDPR

GDPR (and the DPJL / DPGL in the Channel Islands) set out six lawful bases for processing personal data:

1. **Consent**
2. **Contract**
3. **Legal obligation**
4. **Vital interests**
5. **Public task**
6. **Legitimate interests**

Let's explore each in turn.

1. Consent

Consent means an individual has given a clear, informed and freely given agreement to the processing of their data. Under GDPR, consent must be:

- Freely given (no coercion or pressure).
- Specific (covers only the purposes stated).
- Informed (the individual knows what they are agreeing to).
- Unambiguous (usually requiring a positive action, like ticking a box).
- As easy to withdraw as it is to give.

Example:

A small charity runs a newsletter. Subscribers must tick a box on the website form agreeing to receive updates. The charity keeps a record of that consent and provides an unsubscribe link in every email.

Consent is powerful but fragile. If you rely on consent, individuals can withdraw it at any time, and you must stop processing. For this reason, many organisations find that other lawful bases are more practical.

> 📌 **Call-Out Box: Legal Reference**
>
> - GDPR Article 6(1)(a): Consent.
> - GDPR Article 7: Conditions for consent.
> - PECR Regulation 22: Consent required for marketing emails and texts.

2. Contract

You may process personal data if it is necessary for the performance of a contract, or to take steps at the request of the individual before entering into a contract.

Example:

A local gym processes members' names, addresses and payment details to provide access to its facilities. This is necessary to deliver the contract.

A contract is straightforward but narrow. It does not cover activities that are merely convenient. For example, analysing members' attendance patterns to improve services might not be strictly necessary for the contract; it could fall under legitimate interests instead.

> 📌 **Call-Out Box: Legal Reference**
>
> - GDPR Article 6(1)(c): Legal obligation.
> - DPJL / DPGL: Local implementing provisions.

3. Legal Obligation

You may process personal data where it is necessary to comply with a legal obligation. This does not include contractual obligations; it must be a statutory or regulatory requirement.

Example:

A small retailer must keep financial records for tax purposes. An employer must share payroll information with HMRC. A charity employing staff must retain certain HR records under employment law.

Legal obligation provides a clear basis, but only when the law specifically requires the processing.

4. Vital Interests

This basis applies when processing is necessary to protect someone's life. It is intended for genuine emergencies and is rarely used by small organisations outside healthcare or safeguarding contexts.

Example:

A community group calls emergency services and shares a participant's health information after they collapse during an event.

5. Public Task

This lawful basis is available to public authorities or organisations carrying out tasks in the public interest under law. It rarely applies to private businesses or charities unless they are delivering statutory services.

Example:

A school processes pupils' records as part of its duty under education law. A council contracts a charity to deliver social housing services, and processing under that contract may fall under a public task.

6. Legitimate Interests

This is the most flexible basis. It applies where processing is necessary for your legitimate interests, provided those interests are not overridden by the individual's rights and freedoms. It requires a **balancing test**:

- What is your legitimate interest? Do you have an existing business relationship with the data subject?
- Is the processing necessary? Would there be an expectation of the communications?
- Does it override the rights of individuals? Can the data subject easily opt out or unsubscribe from receiving the communications?

Example:

A charity sends postal fundraising appeals to past donors. It assesses that this is a legitimate interest, balanced against donors' reasonable expectations.

For small organisations, legitimate interests can be very useful, but they must be applied carefully. You should document your assessment in a Legitimate Interests Assessment (LIA).

Special Category Data

Some data is more sensitive and attracts additional protections. This includes health information, ethnicity, religious beliefs, political opinions and biometric data. Under Article 9 GDPR, you must identify both a lawful basis under Article 6 and a condition for processing under Article 9.

Example:

A food bank records dietary needs for health and allergy purposes. It relies on Article 6(1)(c) – legal obligation (health and safety) and Article 9(2)(g) – substantial public interest (safeguarding).

> 📌 **Call-Out Box: Legal Reference**
>
> - GDPR Article 9(1–2): Special category conditions.
> - DPA 2018, Schedule 1: UK-specific conditions

The DUAA: Recognised Legitimate Interests

The Data (Use and Access) Act 2025 introduced a major change for UK organisations: the concept of recognised legitimate interests.

Previously, every use of legitimate interests required a balancing test. The DUAA now creates a list of activities where legitimate interests can be assumed, without requiring a test. These include:

- Network and information security.
- Internal administrative purposes.
- Fraud prevention.
- Postal fundraising appeals.

- Certain low-risk marketing activities.

Example:

A small charity can now rely on recognised legitimate interests when sending postal donation requests to existing supporters, without having to document a balancing test each time.

However, this does not mean "anything goes". Processing must still be fair, transparent and limited to what people reasonably expect.

📌 **Call-Out Box: Legal Reference**

- DUAA, Part 2: Recognised legitimate interests.
- ICO Guidance (2025): Clarifies scope and limitations.

Choosing the Right Basis in Practice

How do you decide which lawful basis to use? The key is to identify your primary purpose and choose the basis that most clearly supports it. You cannot switch bases later just because it is convenient.

- If you are delivering a service or contract → **Contract**.
- If the law requires it → **Legal obligation**.
- If it is an emergency → **Vital interests**.
- If you are a public authority acting under law → **Public task**.
- If you have consent and it's appropriate → **Consent**.
- If it is a reasonable organisational purpose → **Legitimate interests (or recognised LI under DUAA)**.

Case Studies: Lawful Bases in Action

Case Study 1: The SME Retailer

A shop takes customer details for online orders. The lawful basis is contract. If it adds customers to a marketing mailing list, that requires either consent (email) or legitimate interests (postal).

Case Study 2: The Local Charity

A charity keeps donor records for tax purposes. That's a legal obligation. It sends postal newsletters under recognised legitimate interests (DUAA). For email newsletters, there must be consent under PECR.

Case Study 3: The Community Sports Club

A club keeps emergency contact details for members. That falls under vital interests. It uses attendance records to improve services under legitimate interests. It keeps financial records under legal obligation.

Conclusion

Every processing activity must have a lawful basis. Choosing the right one ensures you are compliant, transparent and fair. For small organisations, the most common lawful bases are contract, legal obligation and legitimate interests, with consent reserved mainly for marketing and situations where individuals genuinely have a choice.

With the introduction of the DUAA, legitimate interests are easier to use in certain cases, particularly for routine administrative and fundraising activities. But the fundamentals remain the same: be clear, be fair and record your decisions.

In the next chapter, we'll explore accountability in practice - what records, policies and training small organisations really need and how to demonstrate compliance without being buried in paperwork.

Chapter 6: Accountability in Practice

If the seven principles of data protection are the backbone of compliance, then accountability is the muscle that holds them in place. It is not enough simply to comply with the law; you must also be able to demonstrate compliance. Regulators, customers and donors want to see evidence that you take data protection seriously.

For small organisations, accountability might sound intimidating. You may imagine shelves full of policies, reports and legal files. But accountability is not about paperwork for its own sake. It is about having proportionate systems that show you are thinking carefully about the personal data you handle.

This chapter will show what accountability means in practice, the types of records and policies you need, how to train your staff and volunteers and how tools can help keep everything manageable.

What Does Accountability Mean?

The accountability principle is set out in Article 5(2) of the GDPR. It says:

"The controller shall be responsible for and be able to demonstrate compliance with paragraph 1 ('accountability')."

In simple terms: not only must you follow the rules, but you must also prove that you are following them. This applies equally in the UK GDPR, the Data Protection (Jersey) Law 2018 and the Data Protection (Bailiwick of Guernsey) Law 2017.

The accountability principle shapes everything else in data protection. It is the reason regulators ask for policies, data inventories and training records. This is why you need a breach log even if no serious incidents have occurred. And it is why templates, checklists and audit trails matter.

Records You Need to Keep

The most fundamental record is your data inventory or ROPA (Record of Processing Activities). As we saw in Chapter 4, this sets out what personal data you hold, why and how it is used. But accountability extends beyond this.

1. Breach Log

You must keep a record of any personal data breaches, even those you don't need to report to the regulator. This shows you are monitoring risks and taking incidents seriously.

Example:

A volunteer accidentally sends an email with donor addresses visible in the "To" field. Even if this doesn't trigger a regulatory report, you should record the incident, your assessment and the remedial action (e.g., training volunteers to use "bcc").

2. Data Subject Rights Requests Log

Keep a record of data subject access requests (DSARs), rectification requests, erasures and objections. This helps you monitor timelines (you usually have one month to respond) and ensures consistency.

Example:

If an employee requests a copy of their HR file, your log should note the date received, how you verified identity and when you provided the response.

3. Data Sharing and Processor Agreements

If you share data with suppliers or partners, you should have contracts in place. Keeping copies of these agreements, along with evidence that you reviewed the supplier's security measures, demonstrates accountability.

Example:

If you use a cloud payroll provider, you should have a Data Processing Agreement (DPA) that sets out their obligations under Article 28 GDPR.

4. Retention Schedules

Accountability also means being able to explain how long you keep data. A simple retention policy, linked to your data inventory, shows you are not holding information indefinitely.

📌 **Call-Out Box: Legal Reference**

- GDPR Article 30: Record of processing activities.
- GDPR Article 33(5): Obligation to document all breaches.
- GDPR Article 28: Contracts with processors.

Policies and Procedures

Policies do not need to be long or complex, but you should have a small set of key documents. These should be written in plain English, accessible to staff, volunteers and trustees.

The essentials include:

- **Privacy Notice**: Explains to individuals how their data is used.
- **Data Protection Policy**: Sets out your organisation's approach and responsibilities.
- **Data Breach Response Policy**: Explains how to recognise, report and manage a breach.
- **Retention and Deletion Policy**: Sets clear rules for how long data is kept.
- **Data Subject Rights Procedure**: Explains how DSARs and other rights requests are handled.

Example:

A small charity with five staff and 20 volunteers creates a short Data Protection Policy (4 pages), a one-page Retention Schedule and a simple DSAR template. These are uploaded to YourDataSafe, so everyone has access.

> ✒ **Call-Out Box: Legal Reference**
>
> - GDPR Article 12: Transparency obligations.
> - GDPR Articles 13 & 14: Privacy notices for collected and indirectly obtained data.

Training and Awareness

Accountability is not just about documents. People in your organisation need to understand their responsibilities. Regulators often ask for evidence of training when investigating complaints.

For small organisations, this does not mean expensive courses. Short, tailored training can be just as effective:

- A 30-minute induction for new staff.
- An annual refresher for staff and volunteers.
- Scenario-based discussions at trustee meetings.

Example:

A community group runs an annual training session where they work through a hypothetical breach: a lost laptop with member contact details. The group discusses how they would respond, who they would notify and what lessons they would learn.

Keeping a log of who has received training and when helps demonstrate compliance.

> 📌 **Call-Out Box: Legal Reference**
>
> - GDPR Article 39: Role of the Data Protection Officer (includes awareness raising).
>
> - ICO Guidance: Training is a key element of accountability.

Tools for Accountability

Managing accountability records can feel overwhelming, but SaaS platforms make it easier.

- **YourDataSafe** allows you to keep your ROPA, breach log, SAR log and policies in one place. It generates reports you can share with trustees, funders, or regulators.
- **CookieScan** helps with website compliance, ensuring your cookie records and consent mechanisms are kept up to date.
- Simple, secure document storage tools (e.g., encrypted cloud drives) can also help with audit trails.

Example:

A small arts organisation uses YourDataSafe to log three data subject access requests in a year. When a volunteer asks how the charity handles data protection, the manager generates a report showing all requests, response times and training records. This reassures the volunteer that governance is strong.

> ✦ **Call-Out Box: DUAA and Accountability**
>
> The Data (Use and Access) Act 2025 emphasises the importance of proportionate accountability. It simplifies the use of legitimate interests for everyday activities but still requires organisations to keep basic records. The ICO has confirmed that "accountability remains the cornerstone of compliance, regardless of organisation size."

Case Studies: Accountability in Practice

Case Study 1: The Local Café

The café experiences a small breach when a staff rota with phone numbers is left in a public folder. The manager records the breach in a log, reviews procedures and trains staff. When the ICO asks for evidence, the café produces the log and the training notes. No further action is taken because accountability was demonstrated.

Case Study 2: The Jersey Charity

A Jersey charity receives a data subject access request from a former volunteer. Using YourDataSafe, it tracks the request, gathers data and responds within the four-week (Jersey time frame) deadline. The JOIC commends the charity's clear processes during a follow-up enquiry.

Case Study 3: The Guernsey SME

A Guernsey business uses a US-based cloud service. It keeps records of the Data Processing Agreement, the Standard Contractual Clauses in place and its due diligence. When the ODPA audits the company, it praises the proactive accountability measures.

Conclusion

Accountability is about showing your working. For small organisations, that means keeping proportionate records, adopting a few clear policies, training staff and volunteers and using tools to make life easier. By embedding accountability, you not only meet legal requirements but also demonstrate professionalism and build trust.

The next chapter will turn to individuals' rights, what they are, how they apply and how small organisations can respond efficiently without being overwhelmed.

Further Support: Building Accountability through Training

A good accountability framework depends on awareness at every level. If you'd like to ensure your staff and volunteers understand the principles covered in this chapter, you can access an online data protection training course designed for small organisations and charities.

Visit **https://courses.propelfwd.com/gdpr-ci-data-protection-foundation-course** and use the access code **BOOK2025** to get a 20% discount on the listed cost to begin.

Completing the training and recording attendance in YourDataSafe can form part of your evidence of compliance under Article 24 GDPR.

📌 **Call-Out Box: Key Legal References from this Chapter**

- GDPR Article 5(2): Accountability.
- GDPR Article 24: Demonstrating compliance.
- GDPR Articles 28, 30, 33: Records, processor contracts and breaches.
- DPJL / DPGL: Channel Islands equivalents.
- DUAA: Proportionality and legitimate interests' updates.

Chapter 7: Individuals' Rights Made Practical

One of the most powerful features of modern data protection law is the set of rights it gives individuals over their personal data. These rights shift the balance of control away from organisations and towards the people whose information is being used.

For small organisations, individuals' rights can feel daunting. A data subject access request (DSAR) may arrive out of the blue, and suddenly, you are expected to provide copies of everything you hold on a person within one month (or four weeks in Jersey). Or a donor might demand that their details be erased, and you must decide if that is possible without breaking other obligations.

This chapter will explain each right in plain English, highlight what small organisations need to do in practice and provide practical examples of handling requests efficiently.

The Eight Rights Under GDPR

GDPR (and UK/Channel Islands equivalents) provides the following rights:

1. The right to be informed.
2. The right of access.
3. The right to rectification.
4. The right to erasure.
5. The right to restrict processing.
6. The right to data portability.
7. The right to object.
8. Rights related to automated decision-making and profiling.

Each of these must be supported by clear processes, even in the smallest organisation. Let's explore them one by one.

1. The Right to Be Informed

People have the right to know how their data is collected and used. This is delivered through privacy notices. It is a Notice, not a Policy. The difference is that a Notice is an external-facing document and a Policy is an internal document.

Example:

A small charity's website privacy notice explains how it collects donor details, why they are needed, how long they are kept and who they are shared with.

For small organisations, a one-page, plain-English privacy notice is often sufficient. It must be available at the point of data collection, on a website, form, or email.

> ✦ **Call-Out Box: Legal Reference**
>
> - GDPR Articles 13 & 14: Transparency and right to be informe
> - DPJL, Article 12 / DPGL, Section 12: Equivalent local rules.

2. The Right of Access (Data Subject Access Requests, or DSARs)

This is the most common and often the most challenging data subject's right. An individual can ask for:

- Confirmation of whether you process their data.
- A copy of their data.
- Information about how it is used.

You must respond within one month, or four weeks in Jersey. You cannot normally charge a fee unless the request is "manifestly unfounded or excessive."

Workflow for SARs in Small Organisations:

1. **Receive request** (verbal or written).
2. **Verify identity** (especially if sensitive data is involved).
3. **Locate data** (use your ROPA/data inventory to find all relevant systems).
4. **Review for third-party data** (redact where necessary).
5. **Respond within one month, or four weeks in Jersey** (send securely, with explanation of rights).
6. **Record the request** in your log.

Example:

A former employee requests their HR file. The charity uses YourDataSafe to track the request, gather records from its HR system and respond within three weeks. The law states 'without undue delay or no later than one month (four weeks in Jersey).

> 📌 **Call-Out Box: Legal Reference**
>
> - GDPR Article 15: Right of access.
> - GDPR Article 12(3): One-month deadline.
> - GDPR Article 12(5): Fees only in limited cases.

3. The Right to Rectification

If data is inaccurate or incomplete, individuals can request correction.

Example:

A donor updates their email address. The charity must correct this promptly across all systems. This right is straightforward but requires good record-keeping. Using a centralised system reduces the risk of updates being missed.

4. The Right to Erasure (Right to Be Forgotten)

Individuals can ask for their data to be erased in certain circumstances, such as when:

- The data is no longer needed.
- They withdraw consent.
- They successfully object to processing.
- The processing was unlawful.

Limitations: You may need to keep some data for legal reasons (e.g., tax records, safeguarding obligations). In such cases, explain why you cannot erase everything.

Example:

A donor asks for their details to be erased. The charity deletes them from its mailing list but retains a minimal record of the donation for tax and audit purposes.

5. The Right to Restrict Processing

This allows individuals to limit how their data is used, for example, while accuracy is being verified or if processing is unlawful, but they do not want erasure.

Example:

A customer disputes the accuracy of their purchase history. While it is investigated, the retailer restricts use of the data and marks it as "under review."

For small organisations, this usually means pausing certain activities in your CRM or database.

📌 **Call-Out Box: Legal Reference**

- GDPR Article 18: Right to restrict processing.

6. The Right to Data Portability

Individuals can request their data in a structured, commonly used, machine-readable format and transfer it to another controller. This applies where processing is based on consent or contract and is carried out by automated means.

Example:

A gym member asks for their fitness data to be transferred to another provider. The gym provides it in a CSV file.

For most small organisations, this right will rarely apply, but you should be prepared in case.

📌 **Call-Out Box: Legal Reference**

- GDPR Article 20: Data portability.

7. The Right to Object

Individuals can object to processing in certain situations:

- Direct marketing (an absolute right).
- Processing based on legitimate interests or public task (unless you can show compelling grounds).

Example:

A donor objects to receiving fundraising emails. The charity must stop sending them immediately.

The DUAA does not remove this right, even for recognised legitimate interests. If someone objects, you must respect their choice.

> 📌 **Call-Out Box: Legal Reference**
>
> - GDPR Article 21: Right to object.
> - PECR Regulation 22: Absolute right to object to direct marketing by email or SMS.

8. Rights Related to Automated Decision-Making and Profiling

Individuals have the right not to be subject to decisions based solely on automated processing that significantly affect them. This is rare for small organisations, but could arise if you use automated credit scoring or algorithmic decision-making.

Example:

An SME uses an automated system to decide whether to grant customers credit. If a decision is made solely by software, the customer has the right to human review.

Managing Rights in Practice

Handling rights requests effectively comes down to three elements:

1. **Clear processes**: Have written procedures for each right.
2. **Good records**: Keep logs of requests and responses.
3. **Proportionate systems**: Use tools to streamline responses.

Example Workflow for Small Orgs:

- All requests logged in YourDataSafe.
- Requests assigned to a named staff member.
- Deadlines tracked automatically.
- Responses standardised with templates.

This reduces panic when a request arrives and shows regulators that you take rights seriously.

Case Studies: Rights in Action

Case Study 1: The SME Retailer

A customer requests access to their order history. The retailer provides a CSV file within two weeks, meeting the DSAR deadline. The customer is impressed and leaves positive feedback.

Case Study 2: The Guernsey Charity

A volunteer requests erasure of their details after leaving. The charity deletes them from mailing lists but keeps safeguarding records for statutory retention. It explains this clearly, avoiding complaints.

Case Study 3: The Jersey Community Group

A member objects to receiving postal fundraising letters. The group respects the objection, updates its records and ensures no further letters are sent. By logging the objection, the group can prove compliance if challenged.

Conclusion

Individuals' rights are at the heart of GDPR. For small organisations, the key is not to see them as a threat but as an opportunity to build trust. When you respond promptly, clearly and fairly, you strengthen your relationship with customers, donors, staff and volunteers.

With proportionate processes, clear records and simple tools, you can handle rights requests with confidence.

The next chapter will look at data security and breach management, what safeguards you need, what to do if a breach happens and how to reduce risk without expensive systems.

📌 **Call-Out Box: Key Legal References from this Chapter**

- GDPR Articles 12–22: Rights of individuals.
- PECR Regulation 22: Marketing opt-outs.
- DPA 2018 / DPJL / DPGL: Local equivalents.
- DUAA, Part 2: Recognised legitimate interests do not override objections.

Chapter 8: Data Security and Breach Management

Data protection is not only about having the right paperwork. It is also about keeping personal data safe. The GDPR, UK GDPR and Channel Islands data protection laws require organisations to put in place "appropriate technical and organisational measures" to ensure security. What's appropriate depends on the size and nature of your organisation, but doing nothing is never acceptable.

Security failures are one of the most common reasons small organisations come to the attention of regulators. A lost laptop, an email sent to the wrong person, or a hacked website can all cause serious harm to individuals and damage to your reputation.

In this chapter, we'll look at what security measures are realistic for small businesses and charities, what to do when things go wrong and how to demonstrate to regulators, funders and the public that you take security seriously.

What Does "Appropriate Security" Mean?

Article 32 GDPR does not prescribe specific technologies. Instead, it requires "appropriate" measures, taking into account:

- The nature of the data.
- The risks of processing.
- The state of technology.
- The costs of implementation.

For a small café loyalty scheme, appropriate measures might mean using a password-protected CRM and training staff not to share passwords. For a health charity processing sensitive medical data, stronger safeguards like encryption and access controls will be necessary.

Organisational measures are just as important as technical ones. Policies, staff awareness and clear procedures often prevent breaches before they happen.

Practical Security Measures for Small Organisations

You don't need a big IT budget to protect personal data. Many effective safeguards are low-cost or even free.

Access Control: Limit who can see personal data. Use role-based access in systems and avoid shared accounts.

Passwords: Use strong, unique passwords and encourage multi-factor authentication (MFA) wherever possible. Free password managers can make this easier.

Encryption: Encrypt laptops, phones and USB drives that contain personal data. Most modern operating systems offer this as standard.

Backups: Keep secure backups of important data, stored separately from your main system. This protects against ransomware and accidental deletion.

Staff Training: Most breaches come from human error. Short, regular training on phishing, data handling and secure communication can prevent incidents.

Paper Records: Don't forget physical security. Lock filing cabinets, restrict access to offices and shred documents when no longer needed.

Suppliers: Check that your suppliers (cloud platforms, payroll providers, marketing services) offer appropriate security. Always have a written data processing agreement.

Example:

A small Guernsey business uses a SaaS CRM to manage customers. It enables MFA for staff logins, encrypts its laptops and locks its office filing cabinet. These simple steps drastically reduce the risk of a breach.

What Counts as a Data Breach?

A data breach is any incident that leads to:

- **Unauthorised access** (e.g., hacked system, email sent to the wrong person).
- **Loss** (e.g., lost laptop, missing USB stick).
- **Destruction** (e.g., files deleted by mistake).
- **Alteration** (e.g., records tampered with).

Not every breach is catastrophic, but every breach must be taken seriously.

Example:

A volunteer accidentally attaches the wrong document to an email. That's a breach, even if caught quickly. It may not need reporting to a regulator, but it should be logged and lessons learned.

> 📌 **Call-Out Box: Legal Reference**
>
> - GDPR Article 4(12): Defines personal data breach.
> - GDPR Article 33: Obligation to notify regulator within 72 hours if high risk.
> - GDPR Article 34: Obligation to notify individuals if risk is high.

Breach Management: Step-by-Step Workflow

Every organisation should have a simple breach response plan. Here's a proportionate workflow for SMEs and charities:

1. **Identify and Contain**
   - Staff or volunteers must report breaches immediately.
   - Contain the incident (e.g., recall an email, disable compromised accounts, lock down systems).

2. **Assess the Risk**
   - What data was involved?
   - How sensitive is it?
   - How many people are affected?
   - Could it cause harm (identity theft, fraud, embarrassment, discrimination)?

3. Decide on Reporting

- If the breach is likely to result in a risk to individuals' rights, notify the regulator within **72 hours**.
- If high risk, notify affected individuals promptly.
- If low risk, record it in your breach log, but no external report may be needed.

4. Remediate and Learn

- Fix vulnerabilities (update software, retrain staff, tighten access).
- Record lessons learned.

5. Document Everything

- Keep a breach log entry with date, nature of breach, assessment, actions taken and decision on reporting.

Example:

A small charity loses a USB stick containing event attendee lists. The stick was not encrypted. The charity assesses the risk as medium, reports to the JOIC within 72 hours and informs the attendees. It introduces a new policy banning unencrypted portable storage.

> ## ✄ Call-Out Box: Legal Reference
>
> - GDPR Article 33(5): All breaches must be documented, even not reported.
> - DPJL / DPGL: Local reporting requirements (72 hours).
> - ICO / JOIC / ODPA Guidance: Provides breach assessment checklists.

Using Tools for Breach Management

SaaS platforms like YourDataSafe can simplify breach management by:

- Providing a central log for all incidents.
- Offering templates for risk assessment and reporting.
- Reminding you of the 72-hour deadline.
- Storing evidence for audits.

CookieScan also plays a role indirectly: many breaches involve websites, and CookieScan helps keep cookie usage transparent, reducing the risk of "hidden tracking" complaints.

> ✩ **Call-Out Box: DUAA and Breach Management**
>
> The Data (Use and Access) Act 2025 reinforces the accountability requirement for breaches. While the reporting rules remain the sa (72 hours for regulator notification), the DUAA clarifies that sma organisations can take a proportionate approach when assessing low-risk breaches. However, all incidents must still be logged.

Case Studies: Breaches in Small Organisations

Case Study 1: The Volunteer Email Error

A Jersey community group accidentally sends an email to 50 members with all addresses visible in the "To" field. The JOIC is notified within 72 hours, members are reassured, and the group introduces staff training on BCC. No fine was issued because accountability was demonstrated.

Case Study 2: The Lost Laptop

A Guernsey SME loses a laptop containing customer data. Luckily, the hard drive was encrypted. Because the data was unreadable, the risk is low, so the breach is logged but not reported to the ODPA. This shows the value of simple security measures.

Case Study 3: The Ransomware Attack

A UK charity is hit by ransomware, locking its donor database. It reports the breach to the ICO, informs affected donors and works with its IT provider to recover from backups. The ICO commends its prompt reporting and clear communication, avoiding a fine.

Conclusion

Data security is about proportionate, practical measures, strong passwords, encryption, staff training and sensible supplier choices. Breach management is about being prepared: having a simple plan, acting quickly and documenting everything.

For small organisations, regulators do not expect perfection, but they do expect responsibility. By putting in place appropriate safeguards and showing you can handle incidents professionally, you not only comply with the law but also protect the trust of your customers, donors, staff and volunteers.

The next chapter will move to marketing and communications compliance, an area where many small organisations trip up, particularly when it comes to email newsletters, fundraising appeals and cookie banners.

📌 **Call-Out Box: Key Legal References from this Chapter**

- GDPR Article 5(1)(f): Security principle.
- GDPR Article 32: Security of processing.
- GDPR Articles 33 & 34: Breach reporting.
- DPJL / DPGL: Channel Islands reporting obligations.
- DUAA, Part 3: Proportionate accountability for small organisations.

Part 3 - Applying Compliance to Common Scenarios

Focuses on issues you're most likely to face: marketing, third-party relationships and handling sensitive data.

What you'll learn:

Here you'll apply your knowledge to real-world activities. You'll discover how to run lawful marketing, manage suppliers and processors and deal safely with special-category or children's data. By the end, you'll know how to handle these higher-risk situations confidently and proportionately.

Chapter 9: Marketing and Communications Compliance

Explains how GDPR and PECR regulate marketing by email, phone and text and how to gain, record and respect consent using tools such as CookieScan.

Chapter 10: Working with Third Parties

Shows how to choose and manage processors, put proper contracts in place and monitor suppliers to ensure shared compliance.

Chapter 11: Special Category and Children's Data

Covers additional safeguards for sensitive data and for children. Offers practical examples for youth groups, health projects and community initiatives.

Chapter 9: Marketing and Communications Compliance

For many small businesses and charities, marketing is essential. A café wants to email loyal customers about a new menu. A charity wants to send fundraising appeals. A community group wants to text reminders about events. All of these involve processing personal data, and all are tightly regulated.

Marketing and communications is one of the most common areas where small organisations fall foul of the law. Regulators regularly receive complaints about unwanted emails, nuisance calls and misleading cookie banners. Fortunately, the rules are clear once you understand them.

In this chapter, we'll break down the marketing rules in plain English, explain how they interact with GDPR and Channel Islands law and show you how to run effective campaigns that build trust rather than risk fines.

The Legal Framework

Marketing and communications compliance sits at the intersection of several laws:

- GDPR (and UK/CI equivalents): Sets the lawful bases for processing and requires transparency.
- PECR (UK) and the ePrivacy Directive (EU): Add specific rules on electronic marketing (email, SMS, calls) and cookies.
- DUAA: Introduces flexibility for low-risk communications and cookie use.

This layered framework means you need to comply with both GDPR and PECR/ePrivacy. GDPR alone is not enough.

Email and SMS Marketing

Under PECR Regulation 22, you generally need consent to send electronic marketing (emails and SMS). Consent must meet the GDPR freely given, informed and specific. Pre-ticked boxes and "silence" are not valid.

The "soft opt-in" exception applies in some cases:

- You obtained the individual's details in the course of a sale (or negotiations).
- You are marketing your own similar products or services.
- You gave the person the opportunity to opt out at the time of collection and in every message thereafter.

Example:

A café collects emails when customers book online. It may send them offers about future meals under the soft opt-in, provided it gives a clear opt-out.

For charities, the soft opt-in applies to fundraising messages only if the supporter is considered a customer (e.g., someone who bought event tickets). For general donor appeals, consent is safer.

Telephone Marketing

For live marketing calls, organisations can rely on legitimate interests under GDPR, unless the recipient has opted out. However:

- Numbers listed in the Telephone Preference Service (TPS) cannot be called without consent.
- Silent and automated calls are banned without consent.

Example:

A local gym phones former members to offer a discount. If those members are on the TPS, consent is required. If not, legitimate interests may apply, but the gym must respect any opt-out request.

Postal Marketing

Postal marketing is less tightly regulated. Under GDPR, it can usually be carried out on the basis of legitimate interests, provided it is fair and proportionate. The DUAA goes further, making postal fundraising a recognised legitimate interest in the UK.

Example:

A charity sends postal fundraising letters to past donors. Under DUAA, this can be treated as recognised legitimate interests, without requiring a balancing test. However, donors still have the right to object.

> 📌 **Call-Out Box: Legal Reference**
> - GDPR Article 6(1)(f): Legitimate interests.
> - DUAA 2025, Part 2: Recognised legitimate interests (includes postal fundraising).

Cookies and Online Tracking

Cookies and similar technologies (pixels, trackers, SDKs) are regulated by PECR Regulation 6 and the ePrivacy Directive. The rule is simple:

- Consent is required before placing non-essential cookies (e.g., analytics, advertising, tracking).
- Only strictly necessary cookies (e.g., for shopping baskets or login sessions) are exempt.

Example:

A small community group's website uses Google Analytics. It must obtain valid consent before setting the cookie.

This is where many organisations fail. Cookie banners that say "By continuing to browse, you agree…" are not compliant. Consent must be an active choice, with equal "Accept" and "Reject" options. **CookieScan** automates this process by scanning your website, categorising cookies and providing a compliant banner and records of consent. This ensures ongoing compliance without manual effort.

> 📌 **Call-Out Box: Legal Reference**
> - PECR Regulation 6: Cookies and similar technologies.
> - ePrivacy Directive Article 5(3): Consent requirement.
> - DUAA, Part 3: Low-risk cookie exemptions (e.g., certain analytics).

Transparency and Privacy Notices

Marketing activities must always be covered in your privacy notice. This means explaining:

- What data do you use for marketing.
- The lawful basis (consent, legitimate interests, etc.).
- How people can opt out.

Example:

A Jersey SME includes a section in its privacy notice explaining that it uses customer email addresses to send offers under the soft opt-in, with an unsubscribe link in every message.

> 📌 **Call-Out Box: Legal Reference**
> - GDPR Articles 13 & 14: Right to be informed.

Managing Objections and Opt-Outs

Individuals have an absolute right to object to direct marketing under GDPR and PECR. If someone opts out, you must stop immediately. Keeping a suppression list is often the best way. This ensures you don't accidentally re-add them later.

Example:

A donor unsubscribes from a charity's email list. The charity keeps its email on a suppression list to prevent accidental reactivation but does not use it for any other purpose.

> 📌 **Call-Out Box: Legal Reference**
>
> - GDPR Article 21(2): Right to object to direct marketing.
> - PECR Regulation 22: Marketing opt-out rules.

Case Studies: Marketing in Practice

Case Study 1: The Café Newsletter

A café collects emails from customers booking tables online. It relies on the soft opt-in to send offers about future meals, with an unsubscribe link in each email. When one customer objects, the café removes them from the list.

Case Study 2: The Charity Fundraising Appeal

A UK charity sends postal appeals to donors under recognised legitimate interests (DUAA). For email appeals, it collects consent via a tick-box at events. CookieScan ensures its website has a compliant banner.

Case Study 3: The Community Group Website

A community group uses a free website builder that installs analytics cookies. After scanning with CookieScan, it discovers several third-party trackers. It updates its banner to collect consent and updates its privacy notice.

Practical Steps for Compliance

1. Review your marketing activities (email, SMS, calls, post, website).
2. Identify the lawful basis for each (consent, legitimate interests, etc.).
3. Update your privacy notice to reflect this.
4. Implement an opt-out system (unsubscribe links, suppression lists).
5. Use CookieScan to manage cookie compliance.
6. Train staff and volunteers to recognise and respect objections.

Conclusion

Marketing and communications compliance is one of the trickiest areas for small organisations, but also one of the most important. The rules are designed to protect individuals from nuisance and misuse, but when followed, they also build trust and credibility.

By choosing the right lawful basis, respecting opt-outs and using tools like CookieScan, you can run effective marketing campaigns without fear of fines.

📌 **Call-Out Box: Key Legal References from this Chapter**
- GDPR Article 6: Lawful bases.
- GDPR Article 21(2): Right to object to marketing.
- PECR Regulations 6, 21, 22, 23: Marketing and cookies.
- ePrivacy Directive Article 5(3): Cookie consent.
- DUAA, Part 2 & 3: Recognised legitimate interests (postal marketing) and cookie exemptions.
- DPJL / DPGL: Channel Islands equivalents.

The next chapter will explore working with third parties, how to manage suppliers, data sharing and international transfers safely and compliantly.

Chapter 10: Working with Third Parties

No organisation works in isolation. Even the smallest café, charity, or community group relies on others: cloud storage providers, payroll companies, marketing platforms, IT support, or payment processors. Whenever you share personal data with a third party, you remain responsible for ensuring it is handled lawfully and securely.

This chapter explains how to manage third parties, distinguish between data controllers and processors, negotiate contracts and handle international transfers. Done well, this not only keeps you compliant but also reduces risk and builds stronger, more trustworthy supplier relationships.

Controllers and Processors: Who's Who?

A fundamental concept in data protection law is the difference between a controller and a processor:

- A controller decides why and how personal data is processed.
- A processor acts on behalf of a controller, following instructions.

Example:

A charity decides to run a fundraising campaign. It hires a mailing house to print and send letters to donors. The charity is the controller (it decides why data is used) and the mailing house is the processor (it processes data only on instructions).

Sometimes organisations are joint controllers when two parties jointly decide why and how data is used.

Example:

A café partners with a local gym for a joint promotion. Both decide the content, purpose and audience of the marketing. They are joint controllers.

Choosing Suppliers Carefully

Accountability requires that you choose suppliers who can demonstrate compliance. This doesn't mean endless paperwork; it means doing proportionate due diligence.

Practical steps:

1. Ask suppliers about their security measures (encryption, backups, staff training).
2. Check if they hold certifications (e.g., ISO 27001, Cyber Essentials).
3. Confirm where their data centres are located (important for international transfers).
4. Ensure they are willing to sign a compliant data processing agreement.

Example:

A small business uses a SaaS payroll provider. It checks that the provider uses secure UK servers, holds Cyber Essentials certification and signs a data processing agreement. This shows due diligence.

Processor Contracts: What They Must Include

If you use a processor, the law requires a written contract with certain minimum terms. Article 28 GDPR sets these out. Your contract must ensure the processor:

- Processes data only on documented instructions.
- Keeps data confidential.
- Implements appropriate security.
- Helps you meet rights requests.
- Assists with breach notification.
- Deletes or returns data at the end of the contract.
- Provides audits or information to demonstrate compliance.

Most large suppliers have standard Data Processing Agreements (DPAs). For smaller suppliers, you may need to adapt a template.

Example:

A community group hires a local IT company to manage its database. It signs a short agreement requiring the IT company to follow instructions, keep data secure and report breaches.

Data Sharing Between Controllers

Sometimes you share data not with a processor, but with another controller. In these cases, each party is independently responsible.

Example:

A school (controller) shares pupil data with a local authority (controller) for safeguarding purposes.

You should still document the arrangement, especially if sharing is regular. A Data Sharing Agreement can help by setting out:

- What data is shared.
- The purpose.
- Legal basis.
- Security measures.
- Responsibilities for rights requests.

> ✦ **Call-Out Box: Legal Reference**
> - GDPR Article 26: Joint controllers must set out responsibilities transparently.
> - ICO Data Sharing Code of Practice (2021): Best practice for sharing.

International Transfers

If your supplier stores or processes data outside the UK, EU, or Channel Islands, additional safeguards are required. This is because not all countries have equivalent data protection laws.

Adequacy Decisions

The EU, UK, Jersey and Guernsey allow transfers to countries deemed "adequate." This includes places like Japan, Canada (commercial sector) and New Zealand.

Standard Contractual Clauses (SCCs)

If no adequacy decision exists, you must use legal safeguards like SCCs' contractual terms approved by the EU/UK to protect transferred data.

Example:

A small retailer in Jersey uses a US-based SaaS marketing platform. Because the US is not "adequate," the platform must put SCCs in place. The retailer keeps a copy of the contract and records the decision in its ROPA.

> 📌 **Call-Out Box: Legal Reference**
> - GDPR Chapter V (Articles 44–50): International transfers.
> - UK GDPR / DPA 2018, Schedule 21: UK transfer provisions.
> - DPJL / DPGL: Local equivalents.

DUAA: Supplier and Transfer Simplifications

The Data (Use and Access) Act 2025 introduces some helpful clarifications for working with third parties:

- Recognised legitimate interests can cover some routine supplier relationships, such as IT support and payroll processing.
- The Act introduces a new UK framework for smart data sharing, allowing easier switching between service providers while protecting personal data.

- For international transfers, DUAA aligns UK rules more closely with trade agreements, though GDPR safeguards (like SCCs) remain the standard.

Example:

A UK charity using a US cloud service benefits from DUAA streamlining but still documents SCCs in its YourDataSafe ROPA to show accountability.

> 📌 **Call-Out Box: Legal Reference**
> - DUAA, Part 4: Smart data sharing and supplier obligations.
> - ICO Guidance (2025): Practical advice for SMEs and charities.

Using Tools to Manage Third-Party Compliance

Platforms like YourDataSafe help you:

- Maintain a register of all suppliers and processors.
- Store copies of contracts and DPAs.
- Record adequacy/SCC decisions for international transfers.
- Generate supplier compliance reports for funders or boards.

This provides a single source of truth, making it easier to demonstrate due diligence.

CookieScan also plays a role: many third-party cookies and trackers involve international data transfers. CookieScan helps identify these and ensures you capture consent properly.

Case Studies: Third Parties in Practice

Case Study 1: The Payroll Provider

A small café outsources payroll to a UK company. It signs a processor agreement, keeps a copy in YourDataSafe and reviews the provider's Cyber Essentials certificate annually.

Case Study 2: The Fundraising Platform

A Jersey charity uses an online fundraising platform hosted in the US. The platform provides SCCs, which the charity documents. When JOIC asks about international transfers, the charity produces the agreement and its ROPA.

Case Study 3: The Community Group IT Support

A Guernsey community group hires a local IT company to manage its email system. It signs a short processor agreement requiring breach reporting. When the IT company mistakenly deletes some records, the group has evidence of contractual responsibilities.

Conclusion

Working with third parties is unavoidable, but it doesn't have to be risky. By distinguishing between controllers and processors, using proper contracts, documenting data sharing and managing international transfers responsibly, you can meet your legal obligations and protect your stakeholders.

Tools like YourDataSafe and CookieScan make this practical by centralising records and flagging risks.

The next chapter will cover special categories and children's data, two areas where small organisations often deal with sensitive information and where the rules require extra care.

Chapter 11: Special Category and Children's Data

Not all personal data is the same. Some types of information are more sensitive, carrying higher risks if misused or disclosed. For this reason, GDPR and its equivalents (UK GDPR, DPJL and DPGL) create additional protections for special category data and for data relating to children.

For small organisations, these categories can be particularly relevant. A food bank may record health conditions. A youth group may handle children's names and photos. A charity supporting refugees may process data about ethnicity and religion. If you deal with such data, you must apply extra safeguards and take care in choosing lawful bases.

This chapter explains what counts as special category data, how to handle it lawfully and what rules apply when processing children's information.

What Is Special Category Data?

Special category data is defined in **Article 9 GDPR**. It includes:

- Race or ethnic origin.
- Political opinions.
- Religious or philosophical beliefs.
- Trade union membership.
- Genetic data.
- Biometric data (for identification).
- Health data.
- Sex life or sexual orientation.

This type of data is considered more sensitive because misuse could cause discrimination, harm, or significant distress.

Example:

A charity supporting people with diabetes records health details. A school records pupils' religious affiliation for safeguarding reasons. A community centre stores photos of children with disabilities for adapted activity planning.

> 📌 **Call-Out Box: Legal Reference**
> - GDPR Article 9(1): Prohibition on processing special category data unless exceptions apply.
> - DPJL, Part 2 / DPGL, Part 2: Equivalent rules.

Lawful Bases and Conditions for Special Category Data

To process special category data lawfully, you must identify:

1. A lawful basis under **Article 6 GDPR** (e.g., contract, legal obligation, legitimate interests).
2. A condition under **Article 9 GDPR** (e.g., explicit consent, employment law, vital interests, substantial public interest).

Common Conditions Used by Small Organisations:

- **Explicit consent** (e.g., collecting health data for event participation).
- **Employment law obligations** (e.g., recording staff sickness).
- **Vital interests** (e.g., sharing medical information in an emergency).
- **Substantial public interest** (e.g., safeguarding children or vulnerable adults).

Example:

A youth group collects medical information about allergies for children attending a camp. The lawful basis is contract (Article 6(1)(b)) and the Article 9 condition is explicit consent (Article 9(2)(a)).

> ✦ **Call-Out Box: Legal Reference**
> - GDPR Article 9(2): Lists exceptions allowing special category processing.
> - DPA 2018, Schedule 1: UK-specific substantial public interest conditions (includes safeguarding).
> - DUAA: Streamlines "recognised legitimate interests" but doe not weaken Article 9 safeguards.

Handling Children's Data

Children deserve specific protection because they may be less aware of risks, rights and consequences. GDPR recognises this and requires organisations to treat children's data with extra care.

Key Rules:

- Children merit heightened transparency: privacy notices must be written in child-friendly language.
- Parental consent is required for information society services offered directly to children under a certain age.
  - In the UK: under 13.
  - In Jersey & Guernsey: under 13.
  - In the EU, under 16 (member states may lower to 13).
  - Children have the same rights as adults (access, erasure, etc.) and organisations must be prepared to handle them.

Example:

A school offering an online homework portal must obtain parental consent before creating accounts for pupils under 13

> 📌 **Call-Out Box: Legal Reference**
> - GDPR Article 8: Children's consent in relation to online services.
> - DPA 2018, Section 9: UK-specific age of consent is 13.
> - DPJL / DPGL: Mirror provisions.

Practical Safeguards for Small Organisations

For Special Category Data:

- Collect only what is necessary (data minimisation).
- Use secure storage (encryption, locked cabinets).
- Restrict access to authorised staff only.
- Document the lawful basis and Article 9 condition in your ROPA.
- Apply shorter retention periods where possible.

- **For Children's Data:**
- Use simple, child-friendly explanations (e.g., "We collect your name so we can put it on your badge").
- Avoid unnecessary profiling or tracking.
- Always assess whether children would reasonably expect their data to be used in this way.
- Be extra cautious with images and videos, and obtain explicit consent before publishing.

Example:

A community football club keeps emergency contact and medical details for junior players in a secure app. Only coaches have access. Data is deleted when the child leaves the club.

Using Tools to Support Compliance

- **YourDataSafe**: Helps document Article 9 conditions, keep records of parental consents and apply shorter retention periods.
- **CookieScan**: Ensures websites do not use non-essential tracking cookies on children's pages without proper consent.
- **Templates**: Create child-friendly privacy notices and consent forms.

Example:

A Jersey youth group uploads its parental consent records into YourDataSafe. If the JOIC investigates, it can show an audit trail proving explicit consent for health data collection.

Case Studies: Sensitive Data in Practice

Case Study 1: The Food Bank

A food bank records dietary needs (health data) for clients. It uses legal obligation (health & safety) as its Article 6 basis and substantial public interest (safeguarding vulnerable individuals) under Article 9. Records are kept securely and deleted after three years.

Case Study 2: The Youth Group

A youth group asks parents to complete consent forms for allergies and medical needs. The forms are stored securely, and only first aiders have access. At the end of each year, old forms are shredded.

Case Study 3: The Small School

A school records pupils' religious affiliation for safeguarding. It explains this clearly to parents, records the condition under Article 9(2)(g) (substantial public interest) and keeps records until the pupil leaves.

Conclusion

Special categories and children's data require extra care because of the risks involved. For small organisations, this means applying proportionate safeguards: collecting only what you need, storing it securely, obtaining explicit consent where required and keeping clear records.

By treating sensitive information with respect, you not only comply with the law but also reassure parents, donors, clients and regulators that your organisation can be trusted.

The next chapter will focus on **Data Protection Impact Assessments (DPIAs),** a practical tool for identifying and reducing risks before problems arise.

📌 **Call-Out Box: Key Legal References from this Chapter**
- GDPR Article 9: Special category data.
- GDPR Article 8: Children's consent.
- GDPR Articles 5 & 32: Minimisation and security.
- DPA 2018, Schedule 1: UK-specific substantial public interest conditions.
- DPJL/DPGL: Local equivalents.
- DUAA: Digital verification requirements for online services to children.

Part 4 – Building a Culture of Compliance

Helps you embed data protection into daily practice, including when and how to conduct DPIAs and implement governance.

What You'll Learn

Part 4 moves from compliance tasks to culture. You'll learn to assess risk through DPIAs, create proportionate governance, handle international transfers and prepare for emerging challenges such as AI, biometrics and new laws. By the end, you'll know how to make privacy part of your organisation's DNA.

Chapter 12: Data Protection Impact Assessments (DPIAs)

Teaches you when DPIAs are required and how to complete them simply, turning risk assessment into a practical decision-making tool.

Chapter 13: Governance in Practice

Explains how to assign roles, keep oversight and integrate compliance into board or trustee processes so accountability is continuous, not occasional.

Chapter 14: International Considerations

Demystifies international data transfers, adequacy decisions, SCCs and DUAA "smart transfers," with guidance for small cross-border data flows.

Chapter 15: Emerging Challenges and Futureproofing

Looks ahead to technologies reshaping privacy, AI, biometrics, cybersecurity and data ethics and how small organisations can stay resilient.

Chapter 12: Data Protection Impact Assessments (DPIAs)

Sometimes the way you use personal data creates obvious risks. Launching a new app for children, installing CCTV in your community centre, or moving to a cloud platform that stores data overseas all bring potential consequences if things go wrong. Regulators know this, which is why data protection law requires organisations to carry out Data Protection Impact Assessments (DPIAs) for high-risk activities.

At first glance, the idea of conducting an "impact assessment" may sound intimidating, especially for small organisations without compliance teams. But in practice, a DPIA is simply a structured way of asking: what could go wrong, how serious would it be, and what can we do about it? Far from being a burden, a good DPIA can prevent serious mistakes, save money and reassure trustees, donors and customers that risks are being taken seriously.

The Legal Foundation for DPIAs

The requirement for DPIAs comes from Article 35 of the GDPR, mirrored in the UK GDPR, Jersey's DPJL and Guernsey's DPGL. The law says you must carry out a DPIA when processing is "likely to result in a high risk to the rights and freedoms of natural persons." Regulators, including the ICO, JOIC and ODPA, have published lists of situations where DPIAs are mandatory, such as large-scale use of sensitive data, systematic monitoring, or processing that significantly affects individuals.

For small organisations, this most often arises when introducing new technology, handling children's or health data, or using external suppliers that involve international transfers. Even if the law does not strictly require a DPIA, regulators recommend using them as a tool for any project where risks are not obvious.

Why DPIAs Matter for Small Organisations

A DPIA is more than a compliance exercise. It forces you to pause and think about risks before you press "go" on a new idea. For example, a small charity planning to install CCTV in its premises may believe it is a simple security measure. But a DPIA might highlight questions about whether staff, volunteers, or service users will feel monitored, how long recordings will be kept and whether signs explaining the cameras are visible enough.

In another example, a café considering a customer loyalty app may realise through a DPIA that storing customer purchase histories could reveal sensitive habits, that the app developer is based overseas and that safeguards need to be in place before launching. The DPIA does not block the project but makes it safer and more responsible.

Trustees and funders are also reassured by the use of DPIAs. Being able to show that you have considered risks and documented mitigations demonstrates accountability. It signals that you are not only meeting the letter of the law but also applying good governance.

The DPIA Process

Although templates and approaches vary, the DPIA process typically follows four stages:

1. Describe the Processing

Start by setting out what you plan to do. This includes the type of personal data, who will be affected, how the data will be collected and stored and who will have access. Being specific helps identify risks later.

2. Assess Necessity and Proportionality

Explain why the processing is needed and whether there are less intrusive ways to achieve the same goal. A community club may want to take photos at an event to share on social media, but is it necessary to publish identifiable images of children, or could group photos or anonymised shots serve the same purpose?

3. Identify Risks

Consider how the processing could impact individuals. Risks may include loss of confidentiality, unauthorised access, discrimination, or reputational harm. It helps to think about both accidental and deliberate risks, for example, data being stolen in a cyberattack versus staff accidentally emailing the wrong person.

4. Mitigate and Decide

For each risk, think about measures you can take. Encryption, staff training, retention limits, or clearer communication might reduce or eliminate concerns. If high risks remain, you may need to consult the regulator before proceeding.

While these stages can be formalised into structured templates, they are fundamentally about structured common sense.

📌 **Call-Out Box: Legal Reference**

- **GDPR Article 35(7):** Specifies the minimum elements of a DPIA, including purpose, necessity, risks and measures.

Making DPIAs Practical for Small Organisations

One common fear is that DPIAs will be overly complex. In reality, a proportionate DPIA for a small project may run to only two or three pages. The important thing is to show that you have thought through the risks and taken steps to manage them.

Many small organisations keep a simple DPIA template in YourDataSafe, which guides them through the questions regulators expect. By logging DPIAs in the same system as their ROPA and breach log, they create an integrated governance record.

For charities and community groups, involving trustees or committee members in DPIAs can be valuable. It spreads responsibility and ensures decisions are supported by leadership. For small businesses, DPIAs often become part of project planning, ticked off alongside budgeting and marketing.

Case Study: The Youth Club CCTV

A youth club in Guernsey wanted to install CCTV cameras to prevent vandalism. Staff carried out a DPIA using a template. They described the processing (video footage of staff, children and visitors), assessed necessity (balancing security against privacy), identified risks (children feeling monitored, unauthorised access to recordings) and decided on mitigations (clear signage, restricted access, automatic deletion after 30 days).

The DPIA concluded the project was justified, but only with the safeguards in place. The ODPA later commended the club for using a proportionate DPIA to protect young people's privacy.

Case Study: The Charity Health Survey

A Jersey charity planned to run a survey collecting health data from service users. A DPIA identified risks of collecting sensitive data without sufficient security. The charity switched to a survey platform offering EU-based servers, enabled encryption and updated its privacy notice to include the Article 9 (Schedule 2, Part 2 DPJL) condition relied on (explicit consent).

The DPIA not only made the survey compliant but also reassured participants that their sensitive information would be treated responsibly.

DUAA and DPIAs

The Data (Use and Access) Act 2025 introduces some simplifications for small organisations. It confirms that where processing falls under "recognised legitimate interests" (such as routine fundraising or network security), a DPIA is not normally required unless special category data or vulnerable groups are involved.

It also creates a new framework for "smart data projects," where DPIAs are encouraged, but streamlined templates may be provided by regulators. This is designed to reduce barriers for small businesses adopting new digital services while keeping risks under review.

Consulting Regulators When Necessary

If your DPIA concludes that a project still carries a "high risk" even after mitigations, the law requires you to consult your regulator before proceeding. This is rare for small organisations, but it does happen. For instance, if a charity planned to introduce facial recognition technology at events, even with safeguards, the risks might remain too high to proceed without regulator's approval.

In practice, regulators in the UK, Jersey and Guernsey are approachable and often provide informal advice. Consulting early shows good faith and can prevent costly mistakes.

Conclusion

DPIAs are not red tape for the sake of it. They are structured risk assessments that help organisations of any size think ahead, protect people and avoid pitfalls. For small organisations, they should be seen as a practical tool rather than a burden. By describing the project, considering necessity, identifying risks and adopting mitigations, you can not only comply with the law but also demonstrate accountability, professionalism and care for the people who trust you.

The next chapter will look at Governance in Practice, how to put together the policies, roles and oversight that ensure compliance becomes part of daily operations rather than an occasional exercise.

📌 **Call-Out Box: Key Legal References from this Chapter**

- GDPR Article 35: DPIA requirement.

- GDPR Article 36: Regulator consultation for unresolved high risks.

- DPJL / DPGL, Part 3: Channel Islands equivalents.

- DUAA, Part 5: Simplifications for small organisations and smart data projects.

Chapter 13: Governance in Practice

For many small organisations, the idea of "governance" can feel remote, something that belongs in the boardrooms of large corporations rather than in a local café, community group, or small charity. Yet governance is simply about how an organisation is directed and controlled, how decisions are made and how responsibilities are shared. In the context of data protection, governance ensures that compliance is not left to chance or treated as an afterthought.

Strong governance does not have to mean endless policies or a mountain of paperwork. Instead, it is about creating clear roles, proportionate policies and simple oversight mechanisms that embed good practice into daily life. When handled well, governance makes compliance easier, not harder.

What Does Governance Mean in Data Protection?

Governance in data protection refers to the systems and structures that ensure your organisation complies with the law and demonstrates accountability. This includes policies that set out expectations, roles that assign responsibility and processes that monitor compliance.

Think of governance as the framework that holds the seven principles of data protection together. Without governance, policies sit on a shelf, training happens only once, and records are never updated. With governance, there is a cycle of review, responsibility and improvement that keeps compliance alive.

For small organisations, the most important aspect of governance is proportionality. Regulators do not expect a village hall committee to operate like a multinational bank. They do expect, however, that you can show thought has gone into how personal data is handled, that policies are in place and known and that someone is keeping an eye on compliance.

Policies That Matter

One common mistake is to assume governance means creating a policy for everything. In reality, what matters is having a small number of well-written, relevant policies that staff and volunteers actually understand and use.

At minimum, small organisations should maintain a Data Protection Policy, a Privacy Notice, a Breach Response Procedure, a Retention Schedule and a Subject Rights Procedure. These need not be long documents. In fact, shorter, clearer policies are more effective because people are more likely to read and apply them.

For example, a small Jersey charity condensed its Data Protection Policy into four pages, outlining key responsibilities, the lawful bases it most often relies on and how staff should handle subject access requests. The policy was reviewed annually at a trustee meeting, ensuring it stayed relevant. This was far more effective than adopting a 40-page template copied from a larger organisation, which no one ever opened.

The same principle applies to privacy notices. A one-page notice written in plain English can be far more powerful than a dense legal document, provided it contains the required information. The key to governance is usability: documents must guide behaviour, not sit forgotten.

Assigning Roles and Responsibilities

Good governance also means knowing who is responsible for what. In a large organisation, this might involve a Data Protection Officer, compliance teams and legal advisers. In small organisations, responsibility may sit with a single manager, trustee, or even the owner.

Not all small organisations are required to appoint a formal Data Protection Officer. The requirement only applies where processing is on a large scale, involves systematic monitoring, or concerns special category data on a significant scale. However, even if a DPO is not mandatory, it is still good practice to designate a named individual as the "data protection lead." This ensures there is someone who owns the issue, receives training and becomes the point of contact for questions and complaints.

Volunteers and staff should also know their role in handling personal data. This does not mean turning everyone into experts, but it does mean ensuring they are trained to recognise data breaches, understand how to keep records secure and know when to escalate issues. Clear role assignment avoids the common problem of "everyone thought someone else was dealing with it."

Oversight and Review

Governance is not a one-time exercise. Policies, roles and records must be reviewed regularly to ensure they remain effective. For small organisations, this might mean an annual governance review where trustees, managers, or owners run through a short checklist: are policies up to date, is the data inventory current, have there been any breaches or subject access requests, and has staff training been refreshed?

A Guernsey community group introduced a simple system where each trustee meeting included a five-minute "data protection slot." In those five minutes, the committee asked if any requests had been received, whether the breach log needed updating and whether any new systems or projects required a DPIA. This light-touch oversight built a rhythm of compliance without adding heavy burdens.

The DUAA reinforces this principle by encouraging proportionate governance for small organisations. It allows for simplified templates and lighter reporting requirements in certain areas, but continues to

> 📌 **Call-Out Box: Legal Reference**
>
> - **GDPR Article 5(2): Accountability principle.**
>
> - **DUAA, Part 3: Proportionality in governance** requirements for smaller organisations.

emphasise that accountability must be demonstrable.

Using Tools to Support Governance

Technology can help small organisations maintain governance without drowning in administration. Platforms like **YourDataSafe** allow organisations to store their ROPA, breach logs, policies, training records and DPIAs in one place. This not only saves time but also provides an audit trail for regulators or funders.

CookieScan plays a role, too. By scanning websites, categorising cookies and maintaining consent records, it ensures a crucial part of marketing governance is covered without manual effort. Together, such tools make it possible for small organisations to show good governance in practice with relatively little administrative overhead.

Case Studies: Governance in Action

A small retail business in Jersey decided to assign one staff member as data protection lead. She was given two hours a month to update records, review the breach log and check marketing compliance. When the JOIC carried out a routine enquiry, the business was able to show clear records of oversight and avoided any further investigation.

A charity in Guernsey embedded governance into trustee meetings. By adding data protection to the agenda, they ensured that risks and responsibilities were reviewed quarterly. This simple step reassured funders that the charity was well managed.

A UK community arts organisation used YourDataSafe to generate a compliance report for its board. The report showed current policies, a summary of training completed and the status of subject rights requests. The trustees commented that this clear governance information made them more confident in approving new projects.

Conclusion

Governance is the structure that turns policies and principles into real-world practice. For small organisations, good governance means having proportionate policies, clear role assignment and regular oversight. It does not require a compliance department or endless paperwork. Instead, it requires common sense, consistency and a willingness to build accountability into the life of the organisation.

With the right approach, governance becomes a strength rather than a burden. It reassures stakeholders, satisfies regulators and ensures that compliance is not an occasional panic but part of everyday operations.

In the next chapter, we will explore **international considerations**, looking at what small organisations need to know about cross-border transfers, adequacy decisions and the impact of global data protection trends.

> ## ✧ Call-Out Box: Key Legal References from this Chapter
>
> - GDPR Article 24: Measures to demonstrate compliance.
>
> - GDPR Articles 5(2) and 39: Accountability and DPO duties.
>
> - DPJL / DPGL: Channel Islands accountability requirements.
>
> - DUAA: Proportionality in governance obligations.

Practical Tools for Good Governance

Governance becomes easier when you have the right systems in place. The YourDataSafe platform can help you manage your ROPA, breach logs, and policies, while CookieScan ensures your website remains compliant with current cookie and consent rules.

Readers of this book can access both tools at 20% off for the first year using code BOOK2025.

Third-sector organisations automatically benefit from a 50% lifetime discount on YourDataSafe subscriptions.

Find out more at www.yourdatasafe.com or www.cookiescan.com.

Chapter 14: International Considerations

In today's world, even the smallest organisation is connected internationally. A café may use a cloud-based loyalty app that stores customer data in the United States. A charity may raise funds through an online platform headquartered in Canada. A community group may host its website with a provider whose servers are scattered across Europe and Asia. Whether or not you think of yourself as "international," the chances are your personal data already travels across borders.

For this reason, data protection laws do not stop at the water's edge. They recognise that personal data is global by nature and put in place specific rules for transferring information to other countries. These rules are often among the most complex in data protection, but they are just as important for small organisations as for global corporations. If you are not careful, you could find yourself relying on a supplier that puts you in breach of the law without even realising it.

Why International Transfers Matter

The principle is simple: personal data should not lose its protection just because it leaves one jurisdiction. If you collect someone's data in Jersey, they should not lose their rights simply because that data is sent to a server in another part of the world. GDPR and its equivalents require that, when personal data leaves the UK, EU, Jersey, or Guernsey, it must continue to be protected to an equivalent standard.

For small organisations, this most often comes up when using cloud-based services. Many popular platforms are headquartered in the United States, but they process data globally. Even free or low-cost tools can involve transfers, whether it is a newsletter service, a fundraising platform, or an online survey tool.

Understanding these rules helps you choose suppliers wisely, document your decisions and reassure stakeholders that their information is being treated with respect, wherever it goes.

Adequacy Decisions

The simplest way to transfer data abroad is if the destination country has been recognised as "adequate." An adequacy decision means the regulator has assessed that the country offers essentially equivalent protection to GDPR. Transfers to those countries are permitted without additional safeguards.

For example, the EU has adequacy decisions in place for countries such as Japan, New Zealand and Canada (commercial sector). The UK has adopted many of the same decisions. Jersey and Guernsey, recognised as adequate themselves by the EU, follow similar models.

For small organisations, adequacy decisions provide peace of mind. If your charity uses a fundraising platform based in New Zealand, you can rely on the adequacy decision rather than negotiating complex contractual clauses. However, adequacy is limited and can be withdrawn, as the EU's shifting relationship with the US has shown over the years.

Standard Contractual Clauses and Transfer Tools

Where no adequacy decision exists, transfers require safeguards. The most common are Standard Contractual Clauses (SCCs) in the EU and International Data Transfer Agreements (IDTAs) in the UK. These are template clauses approved by regulators that you sign with your supplier.

In practice, many global suppliers already provide these clauses. For example, a US-based email marketing service may include SCCs in its contract with you. Your responsibility is to check they exist, keep a copy and record the decision in your ROPA. For smaller suppliers, you may need to ask directly.

It is not just about paperwork. Regulators expect organisations to assess whether the clauses are effective in practice. For example, does the legal system in the destination country undermine the protections? This is particularly relevant for transfers to the United States, where surveillance laws have been the subject of litigation in the EU.

📌 **Call-Out Box: Legal Reference**

- GDPR Article 46: Transfer mechanisms, including SCCs.

- UK ICO Guidance: IDTAs as UK-specific transfer tools.

Transfers Within Groups and Partnerships

Sometimes international transfers are not about suppliers but about partnerships. A charity might collaborate with an organisation overseas, or a business might share customer data with a foreign distributor. In such cases, you need to apply the same tests: is there adequacy, or do you need safeguards? Data Sharing Agreements and SCCs can be used to set out responsibilities.

For example, a Jersey charity running a joint programme with a partner in Kenya must consider how donor and beneficiary data will be transferred and protected. Even if the partner is small, you, as the original controller, remain responsible for ensuring safeguards are in place.

DUAA and Smart Transfers

The Data (Use and Access) Act 2025 introduced some important changes for UK organisations. It aims to make international transfers easier for small businesses while maintaining protection. Two features stand out.

First, DUAA gives the UK Secretary of State greater flexibility to grant adequacy decisions, often linked to trade agreements. This means more countries may be added to the "safe list" more quickly, though critics worry about lower standards.

Second, DUAA introduces the concept of "smart transfers" for small organisations. This allows certain low-risk data flows (such as metadata or technical support information) to proceed without full SCCs, provided risks are assessed and recorded. The ICO has issued guidance confirming that smart transfers are intended for low-risk scenarios only and must still be logged in accountability records.

Practical Steps for Small Organisations

For small organisations, international transfers can be managed with a few practical steps. The first is to map where your suppliers are located. Many organisations are surprised when they realise how many services involve transfers. A simple supplier register in YourDataSafe can help with this.

Next, check whether adequacy applies. If so, document this in your records. If not, ask your supplier about SCCs or IDTAs and keep copies. Record your decision-making process in your ROPA. This demonstrates accountability if a regulator asks.

Where possible, choose suppliers that offer EU, UK, or Channel Islands hosting options. Many cloud providers now allow you to select a European data centre, which avoids the issue of international transfers altogether.

Finally, review transfers regularly. Adequacy decisions can change, suppliers may move servers, and new tools may be introduced. A light-touch annual review is usually sufficient for small organisations.

Case Studies: Transfers in Practice

A Jersey café uses a US-based loyalty app. The app provides SCCs, which the café stores in its records. The JOIC later reviews the café's compliance and is satisfied because the transfer is documented and justified.

A Guernsey charity runs a campaign using a Canadian fundraising platform. Because Canada is covered by an adequacy decision for commercial organisations, the charity records this in its ROPA and proceeds without needing additional clauses.

A UK community theatre uses a website builder that stores analytics data in multiple countries. CookieScan identifies this during a routine scan. The theatre updates its records, checks the supplier's SCCs and informs website users through its privacy notice.

Conclusion

International data transfers may seem daunting, but with a proportionate approach, they can be managed effectively even by the smallest organisations. The key is awareness: know where your data goes, check if adequacy applies and put safeguards in place where needed. Document your decisions in your ROPA, and you will be well-positioned to demonstrate accountability.

Global data protection is evolving quickly, with new laws emerging in the United States, India and beyond. The DUAA shows how the UK is seeking to balance trade and privacy. For small organisations, the message is clear: you do not need to avoid international suppliers, but you do need to be thoughtful, transparent and responsible.

In the next chapter, we will turn to **emerging challenges and futureproofing**, looking at how small organisations can prepare for new technologies and shifting regulatory landscapes.

📌 **Call-Out Box: Key Legal References from this Chapter**

- GDPR Articles 44 – 50: International transfers.

- UK GDPR, DPA 2018, Schedule 21: Transfer framework.

- DPJL / DPGL, Part 7: Channel Islands rules.

- DUAA, Part 6: Adequacy and smart transfers.

Chapter 15: Emerging Challenges and Futureproofing

Data protection is not a static field. Since the introduction of GDPR in 2018, we have already seen the UK diverge in certain areas, the Channel Islands strengthen their own frameworks, and new laws like the DUAA 2025 reshape the landscape. At the same time, technology continues to evolve, raising new questions that existing laws only partially address. Artificial intelligence, biometrics and digital identity systems are now entering everyday life, even for small organisations.

Futureproofing does not mean predicting every detail of new regulation or technology. Rather, it means adopting habits of governance, ethics and adaptability that ensure your organisation remains resilient as the environment changes. This chapter explores the challenges on the horizon and practical steps small organisations can take to prepare.

Artificial Intelligence and Automated Decision-Making

Artificial intelligence is no longer confined to global tech giants. Even small businesses and charities may find themselves using AI-powered tools, from chatbots that answer customer queries to grant application platforms that score submissions automatically. While these tools can save time and improve efficiency, they also raise compliance issues.

Under GDPR, individuals have the right not to be subject to decisions based solely on automated processing that significantly affect them. This means that if a funding application is accepted or rejected entirely by an algorithm, the applicant has the right to request human intervention. For small organisations, this may mean ensuring that automated tools are used to support rather than replace human judgment.

Transparency is also crucial. If you use an AI system to analyse data, you should explain this in your privacy notice and be ready to answer questions about how decisions are made. Even if you do not understand the technical details, you remain accountable for the outcomes.

📌 **Call-Out Box: Legal Reference**

- GDPR Article 22: Rights relating to automated decision-making and profiling.

- DUAA, Part 7: Clarifies that small organisations using low-risk AI do not normally trigger Article 22, but transparency must still be maintained.

Biometrics and Identity

Biometric technologies are becoming more common, from fingerprint logins on smartphones to facial recognition in workplaces. For small organisations, biometrics might appear through timekeeping systems, security access controls, or even apps used by staff.

Biometric data used for identification is treated as special category data under GDPR, requiring an Article 9 condition. This means you must have a particularly strong justification for processing it. Convenience alone is not enough.

Imagine a small café introducing a fingerprint-based staff clock-in system. A DPIA would likely reveal that less intrusive methods, such as PIN codes, could achieve the same aim. Regulators generally expect biometrics to be used only where strictly necessary, not for minor conveniences.

Digital identity is another growing trend. Governments and regulators are moving towards systems where individuals prove their identity electronically for services, banking, or volunteering. Small organisations may increasingly need to integrate with such systems. Being aware of the privacy implications, such as centralised databases and risks of exclusion, is part of responsible governance.

> ★ **Call-Out Box: Legal Reference**
>
> • GDPR Article 9: Biometrics as special category data.
>
> • DPA 2018, Schedule 1: UK-specific conditions for biometric use in employment.

Cybersecurity and Ransomware

Cyber threats continue to grow, with ransomware attacks affecting organisations of all sizes. Attackers increasingly target small charities and businesses precisely because they are seen as less protected. A ransomware attack can lock your systems, leak sensitive data and threaten your survival.

Futureproofing requires treating cybersecurity not as a technical extra but as a core governance issue. Encryption, secure backups and basic cyber hygiene remain the most important safeguards. But awareness of new threats, such as phishing emails that imitate AI-generated communications, is also essential.

The DUAA emphasises proportionate accountability for cybersecurity. While regulators do not expect small organisations to have military-grade defences, they do expect you to apply appropriate measures and to be able to explain your decisions.

Data Ethics and Public Trust

One of the most significant emerging challenges is not technical but ethical. Laws can take years to catch up with technology, but public trust can be lost overnight. Small organisations, particularly charities, live or die by their reputations.

Consider a youth club using facial recognition to monitor attendance. Even if technically lawful, such a system may feel intrusive and undermine trust among parents. A fundraising charity might use AI profiling to target wealthy donors, but if supporters discover this without transparency, they may feel manipulated.

Embedding ethics into governance helps future-proof your organisation. This means asking not just "is this legal?" but also "is this fair, necessary and respectful?" A simple ethical checklist at trustee meetings, considering dignity, fairness and transparency, can help avoid reputational harm even before regulators act.

Regulatory Change and Divergence

Another challenge for small organisations is the growing divergence between jurisdictions. The EU continues to develop new data protection instruments, the UK is moving in a more flexible direction with DUAA and Jersey, and Guernsey is refining their local frameworks. At the same time, major economies such as the US and India are introducing their own privacy laws.

For organisations that work across borders, this creates complexity. But the fundamentals remain stable: transparency, accountability, security and fairness. By focusing on these core principles, you can adapt more easily to specific local rules.

Funders and partners may also impose standards. A UK charity working with an EU partner may still need to apply EU GDPR rules to satisfy the partnership, even if UK law is more flexible. Anticipating these requirements and maintaining records that show your organisation can meet higher standards will make collaboration easier.

> 📌 **Call-Out Box: Legal Reference**
>
> - EU GDPR (2016/679): Continues to apply in the EU.
>
> - UK GDPR + DUAA: More flexible framework for the UK.
>
> - DPJL / DPGL: Channel Islands frameworks, recognised as adequate by the EU.

Practical Steps to Future-Proof

Futureproofing does not require crystal ball predictions. Instead, it involves building habits of adaptability. Regularly reviewing your data protection practices ensures you stay alert to new developments.

Training sessions should evolve to include emerging risks like AI and biometrics. Tools like YourDataSafe can be updated with new compliance modules, while CookieScan continues to adapt to changes in cookie rules and browser technologies.

Engaging with regulators' guidance is also important. The ICO, JOIC and ODPA frequently publish blogs, guidance and case studies. Subscribing to their newsletters ensures you hear about changes early.

Finally, adopting an ethical mind-set prepares you for future laws. Many new regulations are shaped by public concern. If your organisation already operates transparently and respectfully, compliance with new rules will be a natural step rather than a scramble.

Case Studies: Preparing for the Future

A UK community group explored using AI to allocate volunteers to projects. A DPIA revealed risks of bias if the AI relied on incomplete data. Instead, the group used the tool for suggestions but kept the final decisions with human coordinators. This balanced efficiency with fairness.

A Jersey school considered fingerprint-based lunch payments. Trustees rejected the idea after considering proportionality, opting instead for ID cards. Parents praised the school for its cautious approach, boosting trust.

A Guernsey charity invested in regular encrypted backups after reading about ransomware attacks. When its website was later hacked, it restored data within hours without paying a ransom. The incident reinforced the value of forward planning.

Conclusion

Emerging challenges in data protection are less about predicting specific technologies and more about adopting the habits of governance, ethics and adaptability. Artificial intelligence, biometrics, digital identity, cybersecurity and regulatory divergence will all affect small organisations in the years ahead. By treating transparency, accountability and fairness as guiding principles, you can prepare for these challenges without being paralysed by them.

Futureproofing means recognising that data protection is not just a legal requirement but a way of building resilience and trust. Organisations that approach it this way will be well-positioned to thrive in a rapidly changing digital world.

The final part of this book will bring together these lessons into practical checklists and guidance for action, helping small organisations translate principles into day-to-day compliance.

> ★ **Call-Out Box: Key Legal References from this Chapter**
>
> - GDPR Article 22: Automated decision-making.
>
> - GDPR Article 9: Biometrics as special category data.
>
> - GDPR Article 32: Security obligations.
>
> - DUAA, Part 3, Part 6, Part 7: Proportionality, smart transfers, AI clarifications.

Practical Support for Putting Compliance into Action

Data protection only becomes real when people understand it. To help you put the principles in this book into practice, we've created a short online training course that covers the essential steps for small organisations and charities.

You can access it by using the link and code below for a 50% discount off the listed cost:

https://courses.propelfwd.com/gdpr-ci-data-protection-foundation-course

Access code: *BOOK2025*

Readers of *Navigating Data Protection* also receive a discount on their first year's subscription to our governance tools:

- **YourDataSafe (YDS):** Manage your ROPA, breach logs, and policies in one place. Visit www.yourdatasafe.com

- **CookieScan:** Automate cookie compliance and consent management. Visit www.cookiescan.com

Use the same code *BOOK2025* at checkout to receive 20% off your first year.

Third-sector organisations automatically receive a 50% lifetime discount on YDS subscriptions as part of our support for charities and community groups. Use the code for 20% off your CookieScan subscription.

These resources are designed to make compliance practical, affordable, and sustainable, especially for small organisations that want to build a culture of respect and accountability.

Part 5 – Resources and Tools

Provides templates, checklists and references you can use straight away.

What You'll Learn

This final part equips you with the tools to sustain compliance. You'll create a working toolkit, adapt real examples and build a roadmap for ongoing improvement. By the end, you'll have the confidence and resources to maintain compliance long term.

Chapter 16: Building Your Data Protection Toolkit

Shows how to assemble practical tools, policies, logs, ROPAs, training records, and use platforms like YourDataSafe and CookieScan for efficient governance.

Chapter 17: Templates and Examples

Provides plain-language examples of ROPAs, breach logs and privacy notices to adapt for your organisation.

Chapter 18: Bringing It All Together

Summarises the compliance journey and sets out a sustainable roadmap for continuous improvement and organisational trust.

Chapter 16: Building Your Data Protection Toolkit

Up to this point, we have explored the principles, rules and governance structures that form the backbone of compliance. But understanding the law is only half the story. The other half is having the right tools to put compliance into practice day to day. Just as a carpenter needs a hammer and saw and a café needs cups and a coffee machine, a small organisation needs a toolkit for managing data protection.

The idea of a "toolkit" may sound corporate, but in reality, it is simply the set of documents, records and systems that allow you to demonstrate accountability. The GDPR principle of accountability runs like a thread throughout this book, and a well-constructed toolkit is how you show your working. Without it, you may know you are acting responsibly, but you will struggle to prove it to regulators, funders, or the public.

In this chapter, we will explore what belongs in your toolkit, how to create it proportionately and how digital platforms such as **YourDataSafe** and **CookieScan** can replace messy spreadsheets and ad hoc records with a more structured approach.

What Belongs in a Data Protection Toolkit?

Every organisation's toolkit will look slightly different, depending on size, sector and the types of data it handles. But certain elements are universal. You need a record of what data you hold and why, policies that set out how it is managed, logs that document incidents and requests and evidence that staff and volunteers have been trained.

For some, this may amount to a folder of documents on a shared drive. For others, it may be a cloud platform that integrates governance tasks. The form is less important than the function: can you, if asked tomorrow, show how you are complying with the law?

The Core Documents

The foundation of any toolkit is your data inventory or Record of Processing Activities (ROPA). This is the map of your data, listing the categories of information you collect, why you collect them, the lawful bases relied upon, how long you keep them and who you share them with. Without this map, everything else is guesswork.

Alongside the ROPA, your toolkit should include a Data Protection Policy that outlines your organisation's overall approach, a Privacy Notice that informs individuals transparently and a Retention Schedule that ensures you are not keeping data indefinitely. These are the cornerstone policies that show you take compliance seriously.

A small Guernsey community group, for instance, created a three-page policy that covered responsibilities, breach reporting and subject rights in plain language. This proved invaluable when trustees were asked by a funder how personal data was being safeguarded. The short, clear document reassured them far more than a dense, copied template would have.

📌 **Call-Out Box: Legal Reference**

- GDPR Article 30: Records of processing activities.

- GDPR Articles 12–14: Transparency and privacy notices.

- GDPR Article 24: Accountability obligations.

Logs and Registers

Policies set the framework, but logs and registers show how compliance works in practice. A breach log records incidents large and small, from a lost USB stick to a misdirected email. Even if the breach does not need to be reported to a regulator, recording it shows you are monitoring risks and learning lessons.

Similarly, a subject rights log records access requests, rectification requests and erasure demands, together with dates and responses. Regulators often ask for this when investigating complaints, and it is much easier to produce if you have been maintaining it consistently.

A supplier register is also vital. Many small organisations use dozens of third-party platforms without realising the implications. By maintaining a list of suppliers, where their servers are located and whether contracts include the necessary clauses, you can manage international transfers and processor obligations more easily.

Training Records

Training is a cornerstone of accountability, and regulators often ask how you ensure staff and volunteers understand their responsibilities. Keeping a record of training sessions, attendance and refreshers shows you are embedding data protection into organisational culture.

For a small business, this might be as simple as recording that staff attended a 30-minute annual training session. For a charity, it might include keeping slides or handouts as evidence. Platforms like YourDataSafe allow you to upload and track training logs, making it easier to generate reports for trustees or regulators.

Digital Tools for Modern Toolkits

While paper-based or spreadsheet systems can work, many organisations now find that SaaS platforms provide a more efficient way of managing their toolkit.

YourDataSafe is one example, designed with small organisations in mind. It guides users through creating a ROPA, keeps logs of breaches and rights requests, stores policies and training records and produces reports for governance. By centralising these elements, it reduces the risk of documents being lost or forgotten.

CookieScan complements this by handling the website side of compliance. It scans sites for cookies and trackers, categorises them and provides a compliant banner with consent records. This means you can demonstrate cookie compliance without having to manually update policies every time a third-party script changes.

> ✦ **Call-Out Box: DUAA and Toolkits**
>
> The **Data (Use and Access) Act 2025** encourages small organisations to adopt proportionate toolkits. While it reduces burdens in some areas, for example, by recognising legitimate interests in routine activities it continues to emphasise the importance of maintaining records. The ICO's post-DUAA guidance stresses that toolkits are not optional extras but essential elements of accountability.

Case Studies: Toolkits in Practice

A small café in Jersey kept a simple spreadsheet as its ROPA, updated once a year by the manager. When the JOIC asked for information following a customer complaint, the spreadsheet provided enough evidence to show compliance, avoiding escalation.

A UK charity used YourDataSafe to log subject access requests. When a donor asked for a copy of their records, the charity was able to respond within two weeks, providing a clear audit trail. The ICO praised the charity's governance and took no further action.

A Guernsey sports club used CookieScan to update its cookie banner. When parents asked about online tracking, the club was able to demonstrate that it had reviewed and controlled cookies, building trust among families.

Conclusion

A data protection toolkit is not a bureaucratic burden but a practical aid. It is how you prove that compliance is part of your organisation's fabric, not just a theoretical commitment. For small organisations, the key is to keep it proportionate: a simple ROPA, clear policies, basic logs, training records and supplier registers may be all you need. Whether you use spreadsheets or SaaS platforms, the aim is the same: to be able to demonstrate accountability quickly and confidently.

In the next chapter, we will look at templates and examples in more detail, exploring what a model ROPA, breach log and privacy notice might look like in practice for small organisations.

Chapter 17: Templates and Examples

One of the most common requests from small organisations is not for more theory but for concrete examples. What does a Record of Processing Activities (ROPA) actually look like? How should a breach log be structured? What goes into a privacy notice? The abstract concepts of accountability and governance only become real when you can see them translated into documents that work in everyday practice.

This chapter provides narrative templates and examples that you can adapt for your own organisation. They are not legal forms to copy blindly, but starting points you can shape to your needs. The emphasis, as always, is on clarity and proportionality: a two-page privacy notice that people can actually understand is far more effective than a twenty-page template written in dense legalese.

The Record of Processing Activities (ROPA)

The ROPA, required under Article 30 GDPR for certain organisations but recommended for all, is the map of your data. It sets out what you collect, why, how long you keep it and who you share it with. Without it, you are flying blind. With it, you can navigate subject rights requests, breach management and compliance reviews with confidence.

Here is a simplified example for a small charity:

Charity X – Record of Processing Activities (Extract)

Purpose: To manage donor relationships.

Categories of Data: Name, address, email, and donation history.

Lawful Basis: Legitimate interests (fundraising).

Article 9 Condition (if applicable): Not applicable.

Storage Location: Cloud CRM, hosted in the UK.

Sharing: Mailing house for postal appeals.

Retention: Six years after last donation (in line with tax and audit obligations).

Notes: Donors informed via privacy notice. Objection rights explained.

Purpose: To manage employees.

Categories of Data: Name, address, bank details, payroll information, and sickness absence.

Lawful Basis: Contract (for employment), legal obligation (tax).

Article 9 Condition: Employment law obligations for health data.

Storage Location: HR SaaS platform with EU data centre.

Sharing: Payroll provider, HMRC.

Retention: Six years after employment ends.

A ROPA does not need to be perfect or exhaustive at first. Many small organisations start with a simple spreadsheet. Over time, as projects change and suppliers are added, it grows. The key is to keep it alive; a ROPA locked away and never updated is of little value. Platforms like YourDataSafe provide prompts and structured fields that make maintenance easier, but even a basic document can satisfy regulators if it is kept accurate and proportionate.

The Breach Log

Every organisation experience small data incidents. An email sent to the wrong person, a lost piece of paper, or a volunteer leaving a laptop unlocked. Not every incident must be reported to a regulator, but every incident must be recorded. A breach log is your way of showing that you are alert, responsive and committed to learning from mistakes.

Here is a worked example:

Charity X – Data Breach Log (Extract)

Date: 12 March 2025

Incident: Volunteer emailed donor list to the wrong recipient.

Data Involved: Names and email addresses of 50 donors.

Risk Assessment: Medium - data limited to contact details, but breach of confidentiality.

Action Taken: Recipient contacted, confirmed deletion. Volunteers retrained on BCC use.

Reported to Regulator: No (low risk, contained quickly).

Reported to Individuals: No (low risk).

Date: 2 June 2025

Incident: Individuals: from a staff member's car.

Data Involved: Employee records.

Risk Assessment: Low - laptop encrypted, password-protected, remote wipe enabled.

Action Taken: The IT department confirmed the remote wipe successful. Police report filed.

Reported to Regulator: No (risk sufficiently mitigated by encryption).

Reported to Individuals: No (no risk to confidentiality).

This log shows proportionality in action. Not every breach results in a regulatory report, but every breach is considered, assessed and documented. Regulators in the UK, Jersey and Guernsey have repeatedly said that good breach logs are a strong indicator of accountability.

📌 **Call-Out Box: Legal Reference**

- GDPR Article 33(5): Controllers must document all breaches, even those not reported.

- DUAA, Part 3: Allows proportionate handling of low-risk breaches but requires logs.

The Privacy Notice

A privacy notice is the most visible element of your toolkit. It is where you explain to individuals how their data is collected, why it is needed, how long it is kept and what rights they have. For many people, the privacy notice is the only part of data protection they ever read, so clarity is crucial.

Here is a model example for a small community organisation:

Community Club – Privacy Notice (Summary)

Who we are

We are the Community Club, a non-profit group based in Guernsey that runs activities for local families. You can contact us at [email address] or [phone number].

What data we collect

We collect your name, contact details and payment information when you sign up for activities. If you are a parent, we may also collect your child's name, age and any health information you choose to share for safety purposes.

Why we collect it

We use this information to manage memberships, run activities safely and keep you updated about events. Health information is collected only to keep participants safe and is shared with leaders on a need-to-know basis.

Our lawful basis

We rely on contract (to deliver activities), legal obligation (for tax records) and legitimate interests (to keep you informed about future events). For health information, we rely on your explicit consent.

Who we share it with

We share limited information with our payment provider and IT support. We do not sell your data.

How long we keep it

We keep membership records for two years after you leave the club. Health information is deleted after each activity ends.

Your rights

You have the right to access, correct and in some cases erase your information. You can also object to receiving our updates at any time. Contact us at [email] if you wish to exercise your rights.

Cookies

Our website uses essential cookies to make it work. We also use analytics cookies, but only if you consent via our CookieScan banner.

This notice is short, clear and tailored to the organisation. It avoids jargon and puts transparency into practice. It would usually be backed by a fuller notice available on the website, but the summary version ensures that people can grasp the essentials at a glance.

> ✦ **Call-Out Box: Legal Reference**
>
> - GDPR Articles 12–14: Transparency requirements.
>
> - PECR Regulation 6: Cookie consent.
>
> - DUAA, Part 2 and 3: Recognised legitimate interests and cook exemptions.

Pulling It All Together

These examples show that compliance does not have to mean bureaucracy. A ROPA can be a simple spreadsheet, a breach log, a short table, a privacy notice, or a one-page summary. The power lies not in the volume of documents but in their clarity, relevance and accuracy.

By using platforms like YourDataSafe to maintain records and CookieScan to manage cookie compliance, small organisations can avoid duplication and create a toolkit that is both robust and user-friendly. When regulators, funders, or even curious customers ask about compliance, you can open your toolkit and show, clearly and confidently, that you take responsibility seriously.

Conclusion

Templates and examples bring data protection to life. They turn abstract principles into practical tools. For small organisations, the key is not to overcomplicate them. A clear ROPA, a straightforward breach log and a plain-English privacy notice are often enough to demonstrate strong compliance.

The final chapter of this book will draw together everything we have explored, offering a roadmap for building and maintaining a sustainable compliance culture in small organisations.

📌 Call-Out Box: Key Legal References from this Chapter

- GDPR Articles 30, 33, 12–14: Records, breaches and transparency.

- DPJL / DPGL: Channel Islands equivalents.

- DUAA: Proportionate accountability and cookie flexibility.

Chapter 18: Bringing It All Together

Data protection can seem like a vast landscape of rules, principles and acronyms. GDPR, PECR, DUAA, ROPA, DPIA, the language itself can feel alien, particularly for small organisations that simply want to serve their customers, run community activities, or raise funds for a cause. Yet at its core, data protection is not about bureaucracy. It is about respect. Respect for the people whose data you hold, respect for the trust they place in you and respect for the law that protects them.

Throughout this book, we have broken down that landscape into practical steps. We have looked at why data protection matters, explored the legal foundations and unpacked the principles that underpin everything. We have examined how to build inventories, manage suppliers, handle special category and children's data, conduct DPIAs and create proportionate governance. We have considered international transfers, emerging challenges like AI and biometrics and finally, the tools and templates that make compliance work in practice.

Now it is time to pull it all together into a roadmap for action, one that small businesses, charities and community groups can follow without feeling overwhelmed.

Step One: Understand Your Data

The first step in any compliance journey is understanding what personal data you hold. Without this, you cannot hope to manage it responsibly. This is where the Record of Processing Activities (ROPA) becomes your compass. By mapping your data, what you collect, why, where it is stored, how long you keep it and who you share it with, you gain the clarity needed to make informed decisions.

Small organisations often discover surprises during this step. A mailing list that has grown informally over the years, a forgotten Dropbox folder with sensitive files, or a third-party app quietly storing data outside the UK. These discoveries are not failures; they are opportunities to reset and improve.

The message is simple: start with a map, however rough and refine it over time.

Step Two: Build Proportionate Policies and Processes

Once you know what you hold, the next step is setting out how you will manage it. Policies are the written expression of your intentions. They need not be long or complicated, but they should be clear, tailored and alive. A Data Protection Policy, a Privacy Notice, a Data Rights and Breach Response Procedure and a Retention Schedule are usually enough for small organisations.

Processes put those policies into practice. A breach log, a rights request log and regular reviews are simple tools that demonstrate accountability. Training sessions, even brief ones, show that staff and volunteers know what to do in practice.

Here, proportion matters. Regulators do not expect a scout troop or a village café to adopt the governance structures of a multinational corporation. They do expect, however, that you can show you have thought things through, written them down and acted consistently.

Step Three: Assign Responsibility

Compliance cannot be left in the abstract. Someone in your organisation must take responsibility. For some, this will mean a formal Data Protection Officer, though most small organisations will not meet the threshold. For others, it will simply mean appointing a "data protection lead", a manager, trustee, or volunteer who ensures records are updated, breaches are logged, and policies are reviewed.

Responsibility also means culture. Everyone who handles personal data has a part to play, from the volunteer sending newsletters to the staff member answering customer queries. Embedding awareness and care into everyday practice is more powerful than any policy.

Step Four: Manage Risk Proactively

Risks cannot be eliminated, but they can be managed. Data Protection Impact Assessments (DPIAs) are a structured way of doing this, ensuring that risks are identified and mitigated before new projects launch. Small organisations often find that a DPIA takes no more than an hour or two but saves days of trouble later.

Breaches are inevitable, but logs and response plans ensure they are contained quickly and transparently. International transfers are complex, but supplier registers and contractual safeguards make them manageable. The goal is not perfection but preparedness.

Step Five: Embrace Tools and Technology

Spreadsheets and paper files can work, but they are fragile and easy to neglect. Increasingly, small organisations are finding that digital tools make compliance more sustainable. Platforms like **YourDataSafe** centralise ROPAs, breach logs, DPIAs and policies in one place, while **CookieScan** takes the guesswork out of cookie compliance and international tracking.

These tools do not replace responsibility, but they make it easier to demonstrate accountability. For organisations already stretched for time, technology can be the difference between compliance being maintained and quietly slipping off the agenda.

Step Six: Stay Informed and Future-Proof

Data protection is not static. The GDPR continues to shape European practice, while the UK has begun to diverge with DUAA, and the Channel Islands maintain their own frameworks. New technologies, from artificial intelligence to biometric authentication, are creating challenges that laws are only beginning to address.

Small organisations cannot track every development in detail, but they can stay informed through regulator newsletters, sector guidance and trusted advisers. Building flexibility into policies and processes means you are better prepared to adapt when laws change. Embedding ethics into decisions ensures that even when the law lags behind technology, you maintain public trust.

The Roadmap Summarised

When brought together, the roadmap is clear:

1. Understand your data by mapping it in a ROPA.
2. Build proportionate policies and processes that reflect your reality.
3. Assign responsibility to ensure accountability.
4. Manage risks proactively through DPIAs, breach logs and registers.
5. Embrace digital tools to make compliance manageable.
6. Stay informed and future-proof your organisation with flexibility and ethics.

For small organisations, this is not about ticking boxes but about building resilience. Data protection is not an obstacle to your mission but a safeguard for it. By respecting the data of those you serve, you protect their trust, your reputation and your ability to thrive.

Case Studies: The Roadmap in Action

A Jersey café owner decided to create a simple ROPA after reading about subject rights. The process revealed that customer emails were being stored indefinitely in an old marketing system. By cleaning the list, updating the privacy notice and adopting CookieScan for the café's website, the owner both improved compliance and noticed that customer engagement actually increased.

A Guernsey charity faced questions from a funder about its governance. By using YourDataSafe to generate a compliance report showing its ROPA, breach log and training records, it was able to demonstrate accountability. The funder commented that the charity's approach to data protection reassured them about wider governance too.

A UK youth group introduced a policy requiring DPIAs for new projects. When they considered using a new app for online bookings, the DPIA flagged risks about parental consent for under-13s. The group chose a provider with stronger safeguards, avoiding what could have been a regulatory complaint.

Conclusion: Respect, Trust and Sustainability

The journey through this book has shown that data protection compliance is achievable for small organisations, whether you are a business, charity, or community group. It is not about ticking boxes or drowning in paperwork. It is about respect for the individuals whose data you hold, building trust with your stakeholders and creating sustainable systems that support your mission.

Laws will continue to change, technologies will continue to evolve, and risks will continue to emerge. But the principles remain constant: fairness, transparency, accountability and security. By embedding these into your everyday operations, you future-proof your organisation not just against regulatory fines but against reputational harm and loss of trust.

Your toolkit, your governance, your culture of respect, these are what will carry you forward. And when regulators, funders, or customers ask, you will not simply say "we comply." You will be able to show, confidently and clearly, that you live those principles in practice.

📌 **Call-Out Box: Final Legal Anchors**

- GDPR Article 5: Principles of processing.

- GDPR Article 24: Accountability.

- DUAA: Proportionality, smart transfers, recognised legitimate interests.

- DPJL / DPGL: Channel Islands equivalents.

Epilogue: A Culture of Respect

Compliance is often spoken of in terms of fines, penalties and obligations. While these are important, they miss the bigger picture. At its heart, data protection is about respect. Respect for the people whose details you hold, for the trust they place in you and for the responsibilities that come with stewardship of personal information.

For small organisations, whether businesses or charities, that respect is not just a legal duty, it is a foundation for trust. By being transparent, by handling data with care and by embedding accountability into everyday practice, you show your staff, customers, supporters and community that you value them. That trust, once built, becomes one of your strongest assets.

The journey does not end here. Laws will continue to evolve, technologies will bring new challenges, and expectations will rise. But the principles you have explored in this book will not change. Fairness, transparency, accountability and security remain constant. By making them part of your culture, you have already future-proofed your organisation.

Appendices

Appendix A: Glossary of Key Terms

Accountability - The principle that organisations must not only comply with the law but also be able to demonstrate compliance.

Controller - The person or organisation that decides why and how personal data is processed.

Processor - A third party that processes personal data on behalf of a controller, following instructions.

DPIA (Data Protection Impact Assessment) - A structured risk assessment required for high-risk processing activities.

ROPA (Record of Processing Activities) - A record required under Article 30 GDPR setting out how data is processed.

Special Category Data - Sensitive personal data such as health, religion, or ethnicity that requires additional safeguards.

DUAA 2025 - The UK's Data (Use and Access) Act 2025, which introduced new provisions on legitimate interests, smart transfers and proportionality for small organisations.

Appendix B: Contact Details for Regulators

United Kingdom

Information Commissioner's Office (ICO)

Website: www.ico.org.uk

Helpline: 0303 123 1113

Jersey

Jersey Office of the Information Commissioner (JOIC)

Website: www.jerseyoic.org

Tel: +44 (0)1534 716530

Guernsey

Office of the Data Protection Authority (ODPA)

Website: www.odpa.gg

Tel: +44 (0)1481 742074

European Union

European Data Protection Board (EDPB)

Website: www.edpb.europa.eu

Appendix C: Suggested Further Reading

- ICO Guidance for Small Organisations (UK)

- JOIC Practical Guides for Charities and Small Businesses (Jersey)

- ODPA Guidance Notes (Guernsey)

- European Data Protection Board Guidelines and Opinions

- "Data Protection by Design and Default", ICO guidance on practical implementation

- "The Data Ethics Canvas", Open Data Institute

Appendix D: Sample Resources

Sample Breach Log Entry:

- Date of incident

- Description of incident

- Data involved

- Risk assessment

- Action taken

- Reporting decision

Sample Subject Rights Log Entry:

- Date request received

- Type of request (access, rectification, erasure, objection)

- Deadline for response

- Action taken

- Outcome

Sample Policy Statement (extract):

"We are committed to protecting the privacy and security of the personal information we hold. We handle data fairly, transparently and with respect, in line with the principles of data protection law. All staff and volunteers are expected to uphold these standards."

Practical Resources to Support Your Compliance Journey

To complement the templates and examples in this appendix, you can access our **free online data protection training course** for small organisations and the third sector at https://courses.propelfwd.com/gdpr-ci-data-protection-foundation-course using code **BOOK2025**.

Subscribers to **YourDataSafe (YDS)** and **CookieScan** can also manage their compliance records and cookie controls more efficiently. Use the same code for **20% off your first year's subscription**.

Remember: if you are a charity or non-profit, **YourDataSafe automatically applies a 50% lifetime discount** to your subscription — no additional code required.

Final Words

This book has given you the principles, the laws, the risks and most importantly, the practical tools to make data protection real in your organisation. Whether you are a business owner, a charity trustee, or a volunteer, you now have the knowledge to build compliance that is proportionate, sustainable and trustworthy.

The laws will continue to change, but the culture you build today will carry you forward. Protecting personal data is not about avoiding fines; it is about living up to the trust placed in you. Respect that trusts and your organisation will not only comply but thrive.

Remember:

Information is trust, and trust must be protected.

www.ingramcontent.com/pod-product-compliance
Lightning Source LLC
Chambersburg PA
CBHW071233210326

41597CB00016B/2035